*Controversies in Sociology*
edited by
Professor T. B. Bottomore and
Professor M. J. Mulkay

23
Religion
and Advanced
Industrial Society

# Controversies in Sociology

# Religion and Advanced Industrial Society

JAMES A. BECKFORD

London
**UNWIN HYMAN**
Boston    Sydney    Wellington

Published by the Academic Division of
**Unwin Hyman Ltd**
15/17 Broadwick Street, London W1V 1FP, UK

Unwin Hyman Inc.,
8 Winchester Place, Winchester, Mass. 01890, USA

Allen & Unwin (Australia) Ltd,
8 Napier Street, North Sydney, NSW 2060, Australia

Allen & Unwin (New Zealand) Ltd in association with the
Port Nicholson Press Ltd,
Compusales Building, 75 Ghuznee Street, Wellington 1, New Zealand

First published in 1989

---

**British Library Cataloguing in Publication Data**

Beckford, James A. (James Arthur), *1942-*
   Religion and advanced industrial society.-
   (Controversies in sociology)
   1. Society. Role of religion
   I. Title II. Series
306'.6

ISBN 0-04-301228-0
ISBN 0-04-301229-9 pbk

---

**Library of Congress Cataloging-in-Publication Data**

Beckford, James A.
   Religion and advanced industrial society / James A. Beckford.
      p.         cm.
   Bibliography: p.
   Includes index.
   ISBN 0-04-301228-0. — ISBN 0-04-301229-9 (pbk.)
   1. Religion and sociology. 2. Knowledge, Sociology of.
   3. Civilization, Modern. I. Title.
   BL60.B33 1989
   306.6—dc20                                    89-32418
                                                      CIP

---

Typeset in 10 on 12 point Times and printed in Great Britain by Billing
and Sons. London and Worcester

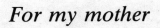
*For my mother*

# Contents

# Introduction

The modern sociology of religion is remarkably self-contained. It has its own concepts, theories and general problematics. It also flourishes in some places as an area for empirical research. But its links with other fields of sociology are, at best, tenuous. As a result, it is rare for studies of religion to be based on, or to influence, broad ideas about the dynamics and problems of today's societies. The main aim of this book is to show how the estrangement between the sociology of religion and other fields of sociology has taken place and what its consequences are for sociological studies of religion.

This book is not an exhaustive compilation of theoretical ideas or empirical findings. Nor is it an account of the state of religion in the late twentieth century. Rather, it analyses the main theoretical currents within which sociological research on religion has been conducted. And it argues that the failure to take the changing character of industrial and advanced industrial societies into account has tended to obscure the fact that, as an object of methodical study, religion remains a puzzling phenomenon – not, however, for the reasons given by many sociologists of religion. For it is not my intention merely to add to the swelling chorus of claims that religion is alive and well in supposedly secular societies. My point is different: it is that modern religion presents sociologists with *theoretical* problems. It challenges many taken-for-granted assumptions about their models of modernity. Religion also represents a challenge to social order in some places and continues to be controversial in many respects.

The central message of this book is that attempts to make sociological sense of present-day religion should take account of theoretical ideas about the distinctiveness of advanced industrial societies and the emerging world order. This necessarily involves a serious consideration of the ways in which ideas about the social significance of religion have changed over time. The pattern that emerges is one of continuity within change. It is questionable, however, whether sociologists of religion have been fully aware of the extent to which their ideas have been grounded in broad theories about industrial society. This book is offered in the hope that a stronger appreciation of these underlying theoretical ideas will lead to a more critical attitude towards them and a greater readiness to modify them in the light of findings from research on advanced industrial or post-industrial societies. Only in this way, I contend, can the sociological study of religion begin to regain the central position that it once occupied in sociology. If this can be achieved, the sociology of the modern world will be considerably enhanced.

# 1
# The isolation of religion

The central argument of this book is that the contours of the sociology of religion have been shaped by specific ideas about industrial society. The sociological questions that have been asked about religion have therefore tended to reflect these ideas. I shall argue that the various meanings and different degrees of importance that have been attributed to such phenomena as secularization, rationalization and the rise of new religious movements are outcrops of underlying ideas about the transition from pre-industrial to industrial society. I intend to criticize these underlying, but rarely examined, ideas.

My main contention is that the legacy of 'classical' sociologists is so coloured by assumptions about the nature of industrial society that attempts to explain the character of religion in a world dominated by *advanced* industrial societies have been hindered. Contrary to much received wisdom and to common sense, I shall argue that religion remains highly problematic for the sociology of advanced industrial societies.

The present chapter will define some of the terms which are important for my general argument and will then chart, first, the process whereby the sociological study of religion moved from the centre to the periphery of sociology; secondly, the broad changes in twentieth century religion which have taxed the explanatory capacity of the sociology of religion; and, thirdly, the factors which have insulated the sociology of religion against, and isolated it from, the influence of wider intellectual debates. The legacy of classical sociology is shown in Chapter 2 to have propelled the modern sociology of religion towards marginality. The argument of Chapter 3 is that the crystallization of general theories of modernization and industrial society after the Second World War led to distinctive but limiting explanations of religion's functional significance. Chapters 4 and 5 examine the responses to these limitations among sociologists who attempted to explain the increasingly controversial aspects of religion in the 1970s. Chapter 6 examines the evidence of a renewed interest in religion as a sociological problem among some Marxists and quasi-Marxists.

We must begin, however, with some brief comments on key terms. First, it should be made clear that the use of 'industrial society' and 'advanced industrial society' is intended to be as general and as inclusive as possible. I am well aware of the very special and diverse meanings that they have borne in the work of thinkers of many different outlooks. I also realize that these terms carry diverse ideological meanings.[1] Nevertheless, I intend to use them in a deliberately non-specific and all-embracing way. 'Industrial society' refers to the kind of social formation that was believed to be emerging in parts of Western Europe and North America as early as the second decade of the nineteenth century. It implies, above all, a shift from agriculture to mechanized manufacturing on a large scale as the dominant means of producing goods for consumption or exchange. It cannot be separated from the decline of age-old communities, the growth of markets and companies based on share capital, the process of urbanization, the emergence of organized labour movements, the consolidation of nation-states as sovereign power holders and the growing impingement of science on all spheres of life. 'Advanced industrial society' refers to the kind of social formation that was believed to be emerging in various parts of the already heavily industrialized world in the 1960s. It is characterized primarily by the growth of world markets in goods and services, the ascendancy of service industries over manufacturing and agriculture, the growth in the numbers and power of multinational corporations, the separation of corporate management from share ownership, the levelling out of social class differentials and the crucial significance of theoretical knowledge and information technology.

For my purposes, these terms are merely convenient labels which signify that competing claims have been made about the general character and determinants of the forms of society which have emerged mainly, but not exclusively, in Western Europe, North America, Japan, Australia and New Zealand. The terms are clearly contestable and are more closely identified with the work of some social scientists than with that of others. But this will not represent a major problem because I shall indicate the precise ways in which the general notions of industrial and advanced industrial society are used in specific theoretical contexts. The main purpose of the terms here is to indicate that the understanding of religion has varied with the kind of interpretations that have been given of transitions to the two most important types of society identified in the past century and a half. In fact, the idea of major transformations in society is itself more significant than the precise labels given to the emerging forms of society.

It is certainly not my intention to suggest that the terms 'industrial' and 'advanced industrial' have any narrowly technological meaning for the character of societies in the late nineteenth and twentieth centuries. On the contrary, as we shall see, none of the major theorists of these two types of society attributes crucial significance to technology alone. Theorists have accounted for the distinctiveness of the two broad types of society in terms of complex sets of very varied factors and circumstances; and, in turn, they have identified widely different implications for religion. The failure to perceive these differences of conceptualization has enabled some sociologists of religion to make the mistake of believing that there was a single (or at least a compound) characteristic of industrial societies which could explain the problems of religion in the modern world.

The concept of 'religion' is no less contestable and variable than that of industrial or advanced industrial society. But, again, my strategy is to conceive of it in such an inclusive fashion that no important contribution to discussions of religious change since the early nineteenth century will be excluded by definition. For my purposes, then, it will be adequate to define religion as concern for the 'felt whole' or for the ultimate significance of things. It can take forms ranging from experiences in the individual person's consciousness to widely deployed symbols of societal identity or even human essence. The advantage of this conceptualization is that it subsumes all narrower definitions without excluding others. In any case, very little turns on the definition that I have stipulated. It will not be employed in claims about the 'real' nature of religion; it will only demarcate the very broad areas of culture and society in which thinkers have located distinctive concomitants of the transition from pre-industrial to industrial society, and from the latter to advanced industrial society.

### FROM INTEGRATION TO DIFFERENTIATION

Religion did not simply become a sociological problem for the first time with the initial wave of sociological classics which appeared in the mid- and late nineteenth century. The problems that arise from the fact that religion is necessarily embodied in social forms had already preoccupied thinkers from the beginnings of civilization. The rival claims of gods and humans; the necessity to store divine wisdom in earthen vessels; and the all-too-human frailties of the priestly representatives of gods – these and many other dilemmas and contradictions are deeply rooted in all major cultural traditions. But it is in the Judaeo-Christian culture spheres that the sociological problems of religion have been most methodically worked and reworked across the centuries. The periods of Late Antiquity, the Reformation and the European Enlightenment are especially important in this respect. It is not difficult to find in them the seeds of ideas and questions which eventually blossomed among the founders of would-be scientific sociology. There is considerable continuity, then, between pre-modern and modern thinking about the social aspects of religion, especially in respect of three broad ways in which theories of modernization have framed the sociological problems of religion.

First, thinkers such as Saint-Simon and Comte regarded much of the content of religious ideas and sentiments as outdated and obstructive to progress, whereas the social functions of religious institutions were considered essential for the more or less harmonious integration of societies entering the industrial era in the early nineteenth century. J. S. Mill, Alexis de Tocqueville and Herbert Spencer adopted similarly functionalist arguments to explain the persistence of religion, although they each had different reasons for doing so. And the subsequent generations of British and United States anthropologists including Edmund Tylor, J. G. Frazer, L. H. Morgan and L. Ward devised still more theoretical reasons for believing that, whereas science had already supplanted magic and religion as a method of understanding events in the world, the socially and culturally integrative functions of religion, myth and ritual still had to be fulfilled if societal stability were to be preserved. A less instrumentalist version of this argument appears in Emile Durkheim's claim that the very constitution of society is by definition a religious process in so far as it involves the establishment of homologous categorizations of people (clans, tribes, nations) and other features of the world (sacred or profane). The argument was that as long as there were societies, the sacred/profane distinction would serve as the symbolic reminder and celebration of individual and collective subjection to them.

Secondly, by contrast, thinkers such as Feuerbach, Marx, and Engels regarded both the content of religious ideas and the supposedly integrative functions of religious institutions as outdated in industrial society and obstructive of socio-political progress. They were among the direct descendants of the anti-clerical, if not actually atheistic, wing of the Continental European and Scottish Enlightenments. They tended to interpret the persistence of religion in both cultural and organizational forms as evidence of deep-rooted resistance to inevitable social change. Their argument was that the human potential for benign development was being frustrated and side-tracked by vestiges of spiritual immaturity in religion. For Feuerbach, the problem was psychological and cultural; human beings had projected their psychological aspirations and uncertainties on to supposedly external powers which then took the form of spirits and divinities with the capacity to control human affairs. His philosophical project was to enable humans to reclaim responsibility for their own world by exposing the psychological origins of religious dependence. Feuerbach's belief was that humans would then become more aware of their common humanity and more capable of devising a just and peaceful social order for themselves.

According to Marx and Engels, religion's persistence was more closely associated with the exploitative and alienating aspects of the class-divided capitalist order; the psychology of projection and dependence was one of the means by which an oppressive social formation reproduced itself. Their aim was therefore to create the conditions for the overthrow of this formation but not in terms of abstract or static psychology. Marx and Engels sought to transform directly the pattern of exploitative social relations to the point where alienation could no longer be experienced and, consequently, religious distortions of reality would supposedly become unnecessary.

A third position was occupied by such thinkers as Max Weber, Ernst Troeltsch, Georg Jellinek and Georg Simmel. In their different ways they each analysed religion as a repository of fundamental cultural meanings through which both individuals and collectivities are able to interpret their conditions of existence, to construct identity for themselves and to attempt to impose order on their environment. Religion is regarded, in this perspective, as a largely symbolic resource or code in terms of which meaning is continuously produced, transmitted and contested. Religion is distinguished from other facets of culture only by the extent to which it provides a warrant for claims to ultimate significance. In some respects, these thinkers tended to regard religion as a kind of cope-stone which locked all the other components of human culture into place – because religious values acted as 'trumps' in the game of culture and/or because the social institutions and organizations of religion had acquired the power to control culture in the interests of powerful groups, classes, or strata.

Despite the differences between these theoretical positions, the approach of sociologists and social anthropologists to the study of religion at the end of the nineteenth century was at least of a piece in its insistence on locating religions in the context of other social processes and structures. They refused to isolate religious from other phenomena. As a result, the sociological study of religion was an integral part of a wider project for understanding the continuities and changes in the very constitution of society at the level of individuals, national societies and 'humanity'. It is as if classical sociologists were, willy-nilly, honouring Marx's epigram: 'The critique of religion is the beginning of all criticism.'

In other words, religion was regarded as an important key to understanding the structures and processes of human societies. For some thinkers, this was because religion necessarily functioned in order to hold societies together. A second school of thought held that it was because religion was the mask which necessarily disguised the 'real' driving forces of societal continuity and change. And a third position regarded religion as a symbolic and organizational resource which could be adapted to suit the interests of particular sections of any society. None of these theoretical positions isolated religion from society's complex web of social relations and processes. Indeed, religion would not have been important for classical theorists if it had been conceptualized as anything other than an integral part of society. As the rest of this book will argue, however, religion became progressively invisible in sociological analysis despite the fact that the classical problematics were never completely dissolved. Only since the 1970s have there been signs of a renewed attempt to make sociological sense of religion in ways which are not constrained by the twin temptations either of regarding everything social as religious or of exclusively identifying religion with formal organizations like churches. At the same time, religion has changed in ways which necessitate a rethink of the widespread tendency among social scientists to disregard its importance in advanced industrial societies and in societies which are affected by them.

One of the major themes of classical sociological theorizing about the social significance of religion, for example, is that the process of differentiation has tended to separate religion from other kinds of social institution. The argument is that, as institutions have become more specialized, religion has been progressively divorced from law, politics, education, economics, etc. The sociology of religion has therefore been marginalized along with its subject-matter. Yet, what has been much less clearly perceived is that the process of differentiation has also taken place *within* the sociological study of religion. Whereas contributors to the founding works of the sociology of religion in the nineteenth century were mainly content to employ all-purpose concepts of religion which treated it as an essentially unitary phenomenon, more recent contributions are usually careful to make distinctions between, for example, religious organization, knowledge, beliefs, emotion, ethics and rituals. In other words, there is nowadays a reluctance to consider religion as a monolith. It has to be broken down into constituent parts or seen from different aspects. The differentiation of religion in society has been mirrored in the differentiation of the concept of religion in sociology. In both cases there has been a shift from a unitary to a partial outlook. One of this book's main objectives is, therefore, to chart the process whereby the sociological study of religion has become separated from the study of other social phenomena.

### FROM INDUSTRIAL SOCIETY TO ADVANCED INDUSTRIAL SOCIETY

At a time when wage labour, the factory system, labour movements, urbanization and the consolidation of sovereign nation-states were all combining to produce radically new types of society in many parts of Western Europe and North America in the late nineteenth century the primary concern of sociologists was with questions of social integration and societal stability. The all-important questions concerned the conditions in which it would be possible either to ensure continuity in patterns of socialization and political order or to achieve a revolutionary transition to a totally different social order. Religion, as the social institution which had previously acted as one of the main vehicles of continuity and stability in older forms of society, was widely thought, by extension, to have crucial significance for the prospects of the nascent form of society. As we shall see, however, the precise character of these prospects varied systematically with the different conceptions of the emerging society.

The predominance of questions about religion's contribution to social integration and societal stability is perfectly understandable in the context of the rapid disintegration or transformation of time-honoured social forms and practices. Religion was variously conceptualized as the key to traditional order, the safeguard of future order, the first obstacle to effective social change and the necessary, but indispensable, casualty of capitalist society. In each case, but for very different reasons, the pivotal role of religion could only be maintained against a theoretical-cum-historical background which made ambitious claims about religion's functions (positive as well as negative) at all times and in all places. The prevailing uncertainty about the nature of industrial (and/or capitalist) society only induced theorists to adopt the kind of postulates about religion's social significance which transcended the limitations of time, culture and space.

The *visions* of industrial society which had inspired Saint-Simon and Comte, and terrified Burke and Bonald, cast religion in a crucial role. On the assumption that it had been the linchpin of the 'old order', religion was believed to be critical for the well-being of future types of society. The most conservative thinkers could hardly conceive of the possibility of a human society without strong religious institutions; many liberal and positivist thinkers were optimistic that certain functions which were indispensable to normal social order could be fulfilled in the future either by modified religious agencies or by religious substitutes; while radical socialists, free-thinkers and assorted anti-clerical parties associated the rise of industrial societies with the downfall of religious organizations and the atrophy of religious sentiment. The great expectations for religion entertained by each of these categories of thinkers were largely conditioned by their respective understandings of the emerging industrial order.

As the contours of industrial society became more clearly defined in the early twentieth century, so the ambitious postulates about religion's functions, transformations and evolution acquired the appearance of even greater solidity. The before-and-after contrasts between what were becoming widely categorized as pre-industrial and industrial societies were used to reinforce either the supposedly timeless functions of religion or its inability to survive separately from the social vehicles, such as traditional communities or extended families, which had borne it across time.

By the 1950s some sociologists were confident that they had indeed identified the key characteristics of industrial or capitalist society. And the fact that the great transformation had apparently taken place without entirely disposing of religious institutions only reinforced the view that the functions of religion must be indispensable to any society. A distinction was therefore made between the *content* of religion (which could be variable) and its *functions* (which had to remain constant). The rising prosperity of many US denominations at that time was also taken as evidence of the enduring qualities of religion in a functionalist sense.

But the declining fortunes of functionalism in the late 1960s and 1970s coincided with a number of major changes in US religious organizations (Wuthnow, 1986). Liberal Protestant churches entered a period of fairly rapid decline in relative popularity, influence and prosperity; the Roman Catholic Church's slow, controversial and uneven drift towards liberalization appeared to accelerate; the first stirrings of a fundamentalist revival were registered among conservative Protestants; the established sectarian movements continued to expand, especially in the Third World; and a bewildering variety of alternative, new and controversial religious movements, many with Asian origins, began to attract attention. The situation in Western Europe, allowing for the different balance between Protestant and Catholic churches, was fundamentally similar, although the speed and intensity of change were both lesser.

These changes did not represent a lethal threat, however, to the functionalist postulates on which the sociology of religion was founded. Rather, they were assimilated into the dominant theoretical framework in the guise of finer and finer differentiations of an increasingly amorphous, yet supposedly universal and necessary, religious institution. The introduction of phenomenological and interactionist perspectives, as we shall see in Chapter 3, made it easier for the functionalist sociology of religion to interpret the changes in religious organizations as adaptive responses to an increasingly complex and varied environment. Diversity in religion was explained in terms of pressures emanating from economic circumstances towards specialization, bureaucratization and professionalization. Parallel developments were taking place in sociological approaches to science, medicine, education and, above all, deviance. As the dominant thinking about industrial society became more confident and elaborate, so previously taken-for-granted assumptions about the functional necessity for such institutions as the family, social stratification, morality and education were questioned – but not rejected. The prevailing response was to acknowledge merely that functional imperatives were experienced differently, perceived differently and 'negotiated' differently in different social contexts. But, if anything, the diversification of experiences and consciousness was believed to reinforce the need for a clearer sense of the underlying social mechanisms for producing and reproducing order in society. The concepts of identity and meaning figured prominently in this theoretical enterprise.

From the mid-1970s onwards, the spiral of intensifying crises in both demand and command economies, the increasing disenchantment in the USA and its military allies with wars against communist insurgents, the emergence of powerful and vociferous social movements of protest against various forms of discrimination and deprivation, the revitalization of moral and spiritual reform movements in the Islamic world and the acceleration of the nuclear arms race all helped to create a mood of despair and fear in industrial societies. Extremisms of various kinds gathered momentum on the left and right of the political spectrum, and religious organizations became embroiled in numerous moral, political and constitutional controversies. The assumption that the logic of industrial society was a benign force which favoured consensual politics, pluralist ethics and anodyne forms of religion had to be called in question (Robbins, 1983). It was no longer enough to acknowledge that religion could mediate the competing claims of diverse interest groups and social constituencies. The reality was that religion could challenge the taken-for-granted basis of social order in democratic or would-be democratic societies. Even more problematic was the charge that extremist religious movements were unfairly availing themselves of the legal privileges and benefits which had been granted to earlier generations of mainly tolerant and democratic churches (Beckford, 1985).

Whereas religion had been widely regarded in the 1950s and 1960s as a bulwark against the potential disorder of industrial society, the situation changed dramatically and ironically in the 1980s. Religion has come to represent a source of disorder in a world increasingly dominated by advanced industrial societies. It is as if the allegedly benign logic of industrialism has turned malignant in its advanced forms. Accordingly, religion is coming to be seen as either a direct threat to the prevailing order, an indirect challenge to its constitutive values, or a declining source of social integration. The direct threat is most clearly associated with fundamentalisms in all the major world religions, while the indirect challenge arises from the growing support for the philosophies underlying, for example, the feminist, ecological, anti-nuclear and psychotherapeutic movements or liberation theologies. The target for most of these threats and challenges is the welfarism and militarism of states which are seen to be increasingly integrated into a world system.

To sum up, late-nineteenth-century sociologists found religion interesting and important for its presumed capacity to supply order and continuity in the emerging industrial society. Mid-twentieth-century theorists attributed to religion the capacity to supply meaning and identity at the level of individuals and groups at a time when the basic orderliness of industrial society seemed to be assured. But the unrest which is characteristic of the world system of states under the domination of advanced industrial societies is beginning to alert social theorists to religion's capacity to threaten or challenge prevailing order.

What this sketch of the linkages between changing conceptions of social order and changing interpretations of religion indicates is that historical contingencies have, paradoxically, inspired claims about religion's allegedly timeless and necessary functions. Thus, speculation about the transformations of

Western societies in the nineteenth century raised questions about the future of religion and gave rise to conflicting answers. But the apparent maturity and normality (if not the inevitability) of industrial society in the 1950s left religion with the task of filling gaps in personal identity and meaning. In a world increasingly dominated by would-be omnicompetent nation-states, religion has again come to present a theoretical problem. Short of adopting the unworthy expedient of arguing that all conflict is eventually integrative, it is not easy to see how the growing frequency of serious conflicts between states and religions can be satisfactorily explained within the parameters of the dominant theories in the sociology of religion. But Chapters 4, 5 and 6 will discuss a range of relatively new ideas about the meaning of religion in advanced industrial or late-capitalist society, some of which offer more plausible explanations of religion's increasingly controversial character.

## FROM CENTRE TO PERIPHERY

The process whereby the sociology of religion has achieved the status of an academic discipline has further contributed towards the fact that religious phenomena cannot be satisfactorily comprehended within most models of industrial society. This is because the sociology of religion has been intellectually insulated against, and socially isolated from, many of the theoretical debates which have invigorated other fields of modern sociology.

### (1) Insulation
Insulation developed, in the first instance, from the fact that, within the perspective of the kind of normative functionalism which set the agenda for much of modern sociology, religion was subsumed in the central value system without regard to its distinctiveness. It was only of interest in so far as it was made to appear indistinguishable from other normative phenomena. To echo Peter Berger's belated misgivings about the normative functionalists' practice of equating religion with other ideational systems:

The specificity of the religious phenomenon is avoided by equating it with other phenomena. The religious phenomenon is 'flattened out'. Finally, it is no longer perceived. Religion is absorbed into a night in which all cats are grey.

(Berger, 1974a, p. 128)

Secondly, the adoption of notions from phenomenological and cognitive sociology in the late 1960s helped to counteract the effects of normative functionalism, but the effect was only further to conceal the distinctiveness of religion in the catch-all of 'meaning systems'. The new approach was successful in showing that religion was a social force which overspilled the boundaries of such formal organizations as churches and denominations. But the corresponding notion of 'invisible religion' was made so all-embracing that it only diluted the specificity of religion still further. The commendable project of revealing the diffuse presence of 'real' religion in society had the ironic effect of turning it into just one meaning system or *Weltanschauung* among others.

A third factor insulating the sociology of religion against the influence of debates about other social phenomena is the time-honoured preoccupation of sociologists of religion with the topic of secularization. The narrow and unremitting focus on the allegedly declining significance of religion (albeit conceptualized in diverse and even conflicting ways) was a legacy of the earliest attempts to capture the distinctiveness of industrial society. As such, it was unquestionably important. But when the discussion of secularization became bogged down in questions about empirical indicators and indexes it lost its articulation with debates about the pattern of wider social changes. Instead, and paradoxically, discussion of secularization had the effect of focusing concern exclusively on to religion itself in isolation from other social phenomena. Moreover, with the consolidation of industrial societies as relatively stable formations in the early twe- :eth century the question of secularization virtually ceased to be of interest to social scientists other than specialists in the study of religion. The continuing focus on the topic within the sociology of religion has therefore had the effect of insulating it against the theoretical preoccupations of the majority of sociologists.

But there are signs that, as I shall argue in Chapter 5, the insulation of the sociology of religion is beginning to be broken down by concern with religion in relation to power of various kinds. In particular, awareness is increasing of the problematic position of religion in the welfare states of the capitalist world order as well as in the developing countries. But this can be achieved only if some of the central components of the classical and revised models of industrial society are radically modified or abandoned.

## (2)  Isolation

To switch from intellectual insulation to social isolation is to take account of the factors which have made the sociology of religion marginal to the rest of sociology.

The first consideration is that, since the academic study of religion was strongly developed prior to the arrival of a distinct sociology of religion, the latter has never been able to assert a monopoly or even a priority over its subject-matter. Unlike, for example, the sociology of deviance, community, or the family, the sociology of religion is a Johnny-come-lately which has never successfully challenged the superior status enjoyed by theology or the history of religions. Indeed, these older and better-established disciplines have, until quite recently, provided the academic training of many sociologists of religion. The result is that the academic status of the specialism has tended to be relatively low because it cannot claim priority over its subject-matter and is competing at a disadvantage with more prestigious disciplines outside sociology.

Secondly, most of the professional associations of English-speaking sociologists of religion have their origins in religious organizations or confessions. The International Conference for the Sociology of Religion has been slowly shedding the imprint of the Roman Catholic Church which fostered its beginnings. The Association for the Sociology of Religion began life as the American Catholic Sociological Society. And the Religious Research Association, which includes scholars from various disciplines, is still recognizably 'religious' in orientation. Only the Society for the Scientific Study of Religion has non-confessional origins but, significantly for my argument, membership is not confined to sociologists. Even more telling is the fact that the American Sociological Association does not at present have a section for the sociology of religion.

The other side of the coin is that the very isolation of, and strong connections between, the professional associations for the sociology of religion have generated high levels of activity and fruitful intellectual debates. My point, however, is that this success has been achieved at the cost of social and intellectual involvement by many sociologists of religion in the debates which have preoccupied most other sociologists. The separate, but overlapping, gatherings of sociologists of religion have been so successful and rewarding for so many specialists that the sociology of religion has drifted away from the mainstream institutions of sociology.

Thirdly, the success of several specialist journals in the sociology of religion is a further contribution to the social isolation of the specialism. It has tended to keep work on the sociology of religion out of the mainstream sociology journals. More seriously, it has helped to foster 'in-house' debates which lack clear articulation with the prevailing interests of other sociologists. For example, debates about religious conversion, the church/sect problematic, civil religion and the dimensionality of religion have all been sustained in ways which, with few exceptions, bear little or no relation to the historical, theoretical, or methodological issues tackled in journals of general sociological interest. The outcome is a form of 'community closure' which is all the more marked than in other specialisms for having occurred at an earlier date and for having had confessional support.

I must add, of course, that the pattern of insulation and isolation is not the same in all countries. It seems to be more pronounced in Britain than in the USA, West Germany, or Japan, for example. But these cross-national variations are minor in comparison to the relatively marginal position occupied by the sociology of religion in most countries. As will become clear in Chapter 2, this marginality has its origins in the particular models of industrial society which preoccupied classical sociology and which had the effect of focusing much mid-twentieth-century sociology on an unnecessarily restricted and restrictive range of topics associated with religion.

Before moving on, however, it is important to emphasize the fact that, despite the marginal status of the sociology of religion within sociology in general, some sociologists take the topic of religion seriously. Yet, they do so as theorists of advanced industrial society rather than as sociologists of religion in the sense that their analyses make remarkably little use of the questions and concepts which have usually dominated the professional meetings and publications of the sub-discipline. Roland Robertson was entirely correct to observe that the 'specialized sociology of religion now confronts an amplification of its marginal status' because 'it is not the sociologist of religion *per se* but rather the sociologist treating religion as part of a larger set of problems who may well be seen as most relevant to the discipline [of sociology] as a whole' (Robertson, 1985a, p. 358). The work of some of these non-specialists represents a return to the problem-oriented approach of classical sociology and a departure from the institution-oriented sociology of the mid-twentieth century. They tend not to study religion for its own sake, then, or in isolation from other phenomena. Rather, they examine it for its relevance to broad questions about, for example, the prospects for revolution, the changing meaning of individuality or the significance of the 'new' social movements.

NOTE

1  See Badham, 1984, for an excellent summary.

# 2
# Religion in classical models of industrial society

This chapter has two main objectives. The first is to examine the various ways in which classical sociologists constituted religion as an object of study in the course of their attempts to specify the character of industrial or capitalist society. The second objective is to raise questions about the legacy of these sociologists' work for subsequent theories of the place of religion in industrial societies.

## SOCIETY REFRACTED BY RELIGION:
## MARX AND ENGELS

The Marxian understanding of religion was distinctive for claiming that the material and social interests of human beings occasioned beliefs in the supernatural or transcendental. A thoroughgoing critique of such beliefs was expected to reveal their social origins and continuing functionality in socially and culturally varied responses to common human predicaments. Confusion and fear in the face of either the terrors of nature or the confusions of social life were said by Marx and Engels to have led to increasingly complex and subtle beliefs in the reality of supernatural powers and divine personalities. The institutionalization of these beliefs and their attendant sentiments allegedly obscured their human *raison d'être* and implicated them in prevailing distributions of power and prestige.

One of Marx's earliest intellectual projects was, therefore, to expose the illusory character of religion, to strip away the distorting layers of religious ideas about social life and to expose the underlying interests sustaining religious institutions. Indeed, the pervasiveness of religious ways of seeing the world was considered to be so strong that the feasibility of the longer-term project of emancipating human potential from systematic oppression was believed to be conditional upon the prior demolition of religion's credibility. Marx gave the impression of thinking that the latter task had been virtually accomplished by various philosophical attacks on religion in the eighteenth and early nineteenth centuries. In his view there remained in principle no religious obstacle to the pursuit of the general emancipatory task to which he devoted his intellectual and organizational energies in the mature years of his life.

Although Marx appeared to turn his attention away from religion in the late 1840s, he had already laid a sufficiently firm foundation for the historical materialist critique of religion to enable other scholars to elaborate on the basic arguments and to apply them in empirical analyses. The diversity of these contributions is too great to be examined in detail here, but it is possible to indicate the broad types of theme which have come to structure sociological accounts of religion in a Marxist vein.

The dominant theme running through Marx's and many Marxists' approaches to religion is a categorical denial of the possibility that religion could be analytically separated from 'the world'. There is no place in historical materialism for anything akin to concepts of an independent realm or transcendental sphere of religion. Indeed, such ideas are dismissed as metaphysical, non-scientific, ideological mystifications of reality. Instead, there is a constant insistence on (1) the possibility of achieving direct and undistorted communal relationships between humans which *could* be symbolized in authentic spirituality and (2) the reality of oppressive social structures, of which religious ideas and sentiments are but a hazy reflection and a subtle mask. Questions about the relationship between religion and the world are answered only in terms of the former's capacity to conceal or distort the latter.

The primary reality of exploitative and dehumanizing social relationships deriving from social class divisions and the detailed division of labour in capitalist societies was not regarded by Marx as a necessarily or even commonly transparent fact. Patterns of unequal power, prestige, or life-chances were believed to be experienced in an alienating and systematically distorted fashion and, consequently, to be represented in mystifying and oppressive forms. In particular, the human authorship of culture and society was said to be concealed by religion in favour of false notions about the dependence of humans on supernatural and sacred powers supposedly external to them. The character of the mystified forms of social consciousness was believed to change with the changing forms of alienation and exploitation. If the latter could be eradicated, religion would have no further reason to exist.

It follows from Marx's depiction of the processes whereby the reality of oppression in society and culture is reflected in, and reproduced by, other-worldly forms of religion that the appropriate method for understanding the roots of this ideological oppression involves the deliberate stripping away of successive layers of putative necessity until the reality of human agency is laid bare. This particular method was prac-tised philosophically by Marx in the transformative 'critique', that is, the continuous inversion of subjects and predicates as they appear in conventional wisdom (Comstock, 1976). The attempt to restore the social basis for human agency and responsibility was regarded as an intellectual prerequisite for practical emancipation from exploitative conditions of life – not as an end in itself, as the 'left Hegelians' might have implied.

It should never be forgotten that Marx's overriding aim was the practical emancipation of people from oppression. This referred mainly to the destruction of social systems associated with modes of production which were dominated by capitalism and secured by the power of nation-states governed in accordance with the interests of the capitalist class. In other words, the oppression which was held to be implicit in systems of social classes was Marx's main target.[1]

In so far as religion was considered an integral part of life in class-divided societies, it came under general attack.

But surprisingly few Marxist scholars have attempted to go beyond Marx's philosophical critique of religion's capacity to mystify, and sometimes compensate for, exploitative social relations. Analyses of particular instances of religious mystification from an historical materialist viewpoint are rare, although the *feasibility* of explaining the precise forms of religion in terms of corresponding social conditions of alienation, division of labour, mode of production and relation to physical nature has not been denied by Marxist scholars. Even more notable by its absence is any attempt to theorize about the kind of non-religious spirituality which might be appropriate to the envisaged social order of communism, of which human praxis, the application in everyday life of science and reason towards progressive and continuous emancipation from irrationality, alienation and oppression, would have presumably become the guiding principle. Lukács and Gramsci, for example, indicated the need for Marxism to go in this direction, and much more recently various liberation theologians have claimed that there is no need to devise a new spirituality because Marx actually promulgated a humanistic, socialistic version of New Testament Christianity. This will be examined more fully in Chapter 6.

For present purposes, the most important consideration is that Marx's unwavering insistence on the need to understand religion in its relation to prevailing features of systematically exploitative and unequal societies lends considerable flexibility to his approach.[2] Indeed, Marx explicitly recognized that religion changes in accordance with social circumstances. This has enabled subsequent generations of Marxist thinkers to draw clear, if contestable, links between perceived shifts in the means of exploitation and changes in the actual expression of religion. As we shall see below, debates among Marxists and Marxisant scholars about the significance of such concepts as advanced industrial society, post-capitalism or post-industrial society have generated varied interpretations of religious change. In this respect, at least, the Marxian legacy has had two different implications.

On the one hand, it has consistently sought to discourage sociologists from taking religion seriously as a feature of social life; but, on the other, it has provided the grounds for a sociological analysis of religion which can be especially sensitive to the changing significance of religion in changed circumstances. It therefore leaves open the possibility that the intellectual problems associated with understanding religion in the mid-nineteenth century do not have to dictate the form of inquiry into religion in the late twentieth century. Nevertheless, Marxist approaches to the study of religion have never enjoyed popularity among specialists in the sociology of religion. Only a handful of specialists have produced explicitly Marxist analyses of religion. In my opinion, however, it is by no means accidental that concern for the specific meanings of religion in advanced industrial society is growing among scholars of a Marxist persuasion. The fact that they tend to be outside the coterie of sociologists of religion as such may paradoxically have something to do with their interest in this topic. It frees them to some extent from obligation to the more orthodox problematics of 'conventional' sociology of religion.

In particular, religion enjoys no special privileges in historical materialism. Engels suggested that it may have been natural to be religious in prehistoric times but that, with the advent of sophisticated cultures, religion became either unnecessary or an expression of the special forms of alienation characteristic of class-divided capitalist societies. It forms part of ideology and, as such, has often been employed in the defence and promotion of ruling material interests. It has also served the interest of rebellious elements from time to time – but only as an opiate or a rallying cry in the short term. The significance of the capitalist mode of production and of industrial forms of productive organization lies in their capacity to intensify exploitation and alienation whilst, paradoxically, preparing the way for a revolution and a dictatorship of the proletariat. In this sense, industrial (or, more commonly, capitalist) society is regarded as a problem rather than as a solution: not because of any inherent fault of technology or manufacturing processes, but rather because of the necessarily contradictory character of social relations between capital and labour which has shaped industrial society. This is the factor which, according to Marx, explains the dynamics and the downfall of the capitalist mode of production.

Religion is of interest, then, mainly for its capacity to shield people from these harsh realities and to bolster the prevailing distributions of power in society by making them appear to be natural and/or necessary. In this respect, it matters little whether the result is achieved by an ideology dominant over the whole society or by an ethos which merely prevents members of ruling groups from abandoning their commitment to the social order (Turner, 1983). As has often been remarked, historical materialist interpretations of religion have also tended to be focused on its capacity to glorify and therefore to reproduce prevailing social order in symbolic form. By contrast, Marxists' concern with the concrete institutions and organizations of religion has been very weak. The ideological dimension is regarded as all-important and is the necessary counterpart to the very strong claims made by historical materialists about the systemic structure of human societies. It is the mechanism which explains the reproductive, constraining and self-equilibrating aspects of the system. This is the primary context in which religion could be said to be of interest to Marxist thinkers. The degree of dependence on ideas specifically about industrial societies is relatively low, but the putative nature of the capitalist mode of production is nevertheless of immense importance in this perspective.

The formative writings of Marx and Engels have dictated a highly distinctive agenda for the sociology of religion. There has been a continuing interest in the functions fulfilled by religion in pre-capitalist societies and in aspects of the transition from feudalism to capitalism. These topics have been important partly because they raise the prospect of non-alienated forms of religion either in relatively non-exploitative social conditions or in the context of rebellions against increasingly exploitative conditions.

The Austro-Marxists, Otto Bauer (1927) and Max Adler (1925), were among the first to develop these possibilities and to distance themselves from the rigid materialism of the mature Engels and his Bolshevik successors such as Plekhanov,

Lenin and Bukharin. Yet, despite the deep philosophical and political differences which divided all these inheritors of the legacy of Marx and Engels, there was also a remarkable degree of agreement among them on the importance of explaining (away) the origins of religion.

The other side of this coin is the preoccupation, especially in state socialist societies based on Marxist principles, with the persistence of religion in circumstances which, in theory, should have dispensed with it. The response of many sociologists of religion in Eastern Europe, for example, has been to regard religion as a practice which persists only in marginal populations which are inadequately integrated into the socialist framework (Vrcan, 1977). Similarly, participants in religiously inspired movements of rebellion against imperial powers in Third World countries are believed to be marginal and consequently temporary protesters against integration into the predominantly capitalist world economic system (Lanternari, 1963).

The third legacy of Marx and Engels's interpretation of the dynamics of capitalism and industrial society has been a protracted debate about the extent to which religion enjoys autonomy from the economic base of society. The notion of the relative autonomy of the superstructure has encouraged some sociologists to acknowledge that religion could be, in certain circumstances, an authentic expression of resistance against class-based exploitation and oppression (Maduro, 1977). As we shall see in Chapter 5, however, some exponents of 'structuralist Marxism' have also argued that there might be a continuing need for religion in all social systems – including communist societies.

These three items on the agenda of a mainstream Marxist sociology of religion reflect the predominance of Marx and Engels's particular understanding of capitalism and industrial society. A strongly evolutionist perspective runs through each item, even though the need to take account of the positive, albeit temporary, significance of religion as an agent of constructive rebellion or resistance among people marginalized by the master principles of capitalism, industrialism, imperialism and colonialism is acknowledged. Consequently, the ultimately epiphenomenal status of religion is repeatedly asserted even in relation to contexts where religion may appear to be the dominant force. Religion was not expected to outlast the inner contradictions of capitalism.

## SOCIETY AS RELIGIOUS: DURKHEIM

Some of Durkheim's famous aphorisms can be misleading. For example, 'society worships itself' does not mean that the specific groups, institutions and processes which comprise a society at any instant are the object of veneration. The meaning is pitched on a much higher level of abstraction and generality. Durkheim's claim is actually that religion is a positive response to the very sociality of social life. In other words, religion sacralizes the fact and manner of human bonding as a prerequisite for any particular form of society. A more precise rendering of the aphorism would be that religion celebrates, and thereby reinforces, the fact that people can form societies.

If it is the potential for sociality which is the object of religion according to Durkheim, how can this be reconciled with his celebrated categorial distinction between the sacred and the profane? How can this distinction be central to religion? The answer is that the sacred represents things which have the capacity to bind people together into a society, whereas the profane represents things which are unrelated to the very possibility of society. It follows from this interpretation that the difference between religion and morality is reduced, for they both arise from the alleged needs of a society to ensure that the possibility of social solidarity should be maintained and protected. This is, after all, not surprising in view of Durkheim's beliefs that religion binds people together in a moral community and that whatever promotes social solidarity is also moral. The distinction may be merely functional; religion symbolizes sociality as the ground of all social life, while morality codifies and regulates action in everyday life.

An important consequence of associating the sacred with people, things and practices which symbolize the very possibility of life in society is that the decline or disappearance of religion is rendered virtually inconceivable except in the case of a societal collapse or destruction. Durkheim, in contrast to many of his contemporaries, eschewed speculation about secularization in the most widely accepted senses of the term. He certainly believed that religious *institutions* had been declining in power since prehistoric times and that the rate of decline had accelerated in industrialized societies, but it did not follow for him that the *functions* which had traditionally been fulfilled by religion were also in decline. Many areas of social life had unquestionably been freed from the control of religious institutions, but he insisted that there was still a need for basic sociality to be symbolized, codified, experienced and celebrated. It is significant that his understanding of the largely 'facilitative' notion of the sacred led him to examine the changes which might occur in the modalities of religion. That is, he envisaged the probability that, with increasing rates of moral density, geographical mobility and social differentiation, the individual person would come increasingly to be a symbol of the fundamental grounds of sociality. The older religious symbols had primarily celebrated the value of various *collectivities* such as households, churches, tribes or clans. Durkheim anticipated, however, that sacredness would eventually be located in *individual* persons because it would be precisely by means of their individuality, and consequently of their interdependence, that they would be accounted members in good standing of their society. Social integration and solidarity would therefore come to be conceptualized in terms of the bonding between increasingly autonomous but interdependent individuals, and this would be reflected in correspondingly individualized symbols of the sacred.

It needs to be stressed that Durkheim's sketch of the resultant 'cult of man' was very different from Comte's religion of humanity because, among other things, the former was based on ideas about the sacredness attributed to each person separately, whereas the latter was based on an abstract, timeless and basically asocial conception of generic humanity. Durkheim's cult of man was expected to enthuse and to constrain its devotees by moral suasion, but the controlling function of Comte's religion of humanity was centred on medieval rituals, liturgies and calendars which were rooted in collectivist symbolism. But collective representations, according to Durkheim, were already losing their sway over people's thinking and feeling in industrial society. It was left, then, to the symbols of sacred individuality paradoxically to codify the solidarity peculiar to modern societies. They were expected to carry in coded form the solution to the conundrum at the centre of Durkheim's major preoccupation: 'Why does the individual, while becoming more autonomous, depend more upon society? How can [the individual] be at once more individual and more solidary?' (Durkheim, 1964, p. 37). The answer was that it is by means of symbols of the sacred in each individual that society's capacity to impose obligatory patterns of action could be preserved.

The 'problem' of religion in industrial society for Durkheim was not that it was in danger of disappearing or of being compromised with 'the world'. It was, instead, a problem about the pace of change in religious symbolism. If new symbols of sacred individuality could be smoothly adopted and embodied in, for example, new forms of ritual and codes of morality, the problem would be solved. But if habits of thought based on representations of the collectivity as sacred in itself persisted, religious institutions would jeopardise their capacity to influence social life. The problem would then be that rapid social change would be unchecked by normative considerations, with serious consequences for the level of anomie.

In contrast to many of his contemporaries, Durkheim could contemplate with equanimity the prospect of secularization in the sense of the declining capacity of formal religious organizations to influence the course of social life. This was not the problem of religion. The real problem was to ensure that the institutions of religion did not delay the demise of outmoded collective representations and did not resist the dissemination of more appropriate symbols of social solidarity based on notions of the sacredness inherent in each person. Difficulties were expected to arise from any failure of religious institutions to keep pace with the rapidly changing character of social relations in all other spheres of life. This was not so much a problem of the relation between religion and 'the world', since Durkheim adamantly refused to separate them in these oppositional terms, as it was a problem of the synchronization of changes in various social institutions.

This was especially true of relations between the institution of science and other features of society. Rationalist though he was, Durkheim did not believe that science and critical reason were necessarily bound to diminish the importance of the religious function. In fact, he actively promoted the dissemination of scientific ideas about matters such as morality which had previously been controlled by religious organizations – but only in order to dispense with what he considered to be outdated mystifications and dogmas. His view was that science, properly produced, regulated and understood, would undermine faith in unsupported meta-physical abstractions without leaving a dangerous vacuum. Science was confidently expected to provide the basis for a new morality and spirituality which would eventually function as guarantors of ultimate meaning and identity. There was no inherent contradiction in Durkheim's mind between reason and the religious function: only between reactionary religious organizations and empirically grounded scientific truths. In this respect, Durkheim's version of industrial society drew at least as heavily on the positivisms of Saint-Simon, Comte and Spencer as on the rationalism of the French Enlightenment.

Religion was of the utmost importance for Durkheim because it was considered to be the mechanism which gener-ated symbols of the very basis on which it was possible for all aspects of social life to proceed in relative harmony. A society without religion was therefore unthinkable for Durkheim, in the sense that no society could survive unless it had some means of 'thinking' about itself as a society. The function of religion is consequently said to be to make society possible.

Durkheim's claim that society has the capacity to 'think about itself' may seem mystifying. What was meant is that reflections on social action are an integral part of society. A social action involves varying degrees of self-reflection. Society, as a more or less self-contained sphere of patterned actions, possesses its own collective ways of reflecting on itself

– religion and morality, or what Durkheim (1964) termed 'hyperspirituality'. They are double-edged phenomena in the sense of *representing* the state of affairs and of *regulating* it at the same time. But this is achieved primarily by means of ritual and codes of obligation: not rational thought. Again, the crucial consideration for Durkheim was whether the contents of ritual and morality could continue to correspond with the changing character of social relationships in all spheres of social life. The functional necessity for religion, ritual and morality was never in doubt, but the question of their form and content preoccupied Durkheim and his followers.

More highly individualized ideas of the person were considered by Durkheim to be not only *appropriate* to an age in which the division of labour was rapidly becoming more and more complex and in which the moral density of societies was undermining the old, particularistic boundaries between formerly separate socio-cultural groups but also *essential* for the preservation of social order. The modal figure of the individual, as a symbol of sacredness, was therefore believed to be *imposed* by society in pursuit of its own ends. The philosophy of individualism and the existential experience of individuality were not therefore seen as evidence of a regrettable departure from, or corruptions of, an earlier and preferable state of society. They were regarded as adaptations to changing circumstances – no less real and no more avoidable than the growth of manufacturing industry or the production of 'normal' rates of crime. As a result, neither pathos nor romanticism attaches to Durkheim's account of the emergence of individuality in industrial society.[3]

Indeed, it could be argued that much of Durkheim's optimism stemmed from his belief that it would be precisely by means of images about the sacred qualities of the individual person that universalistic ethics would progress and that, concomitantly, particularism would decline. The implication was that legal and moral systems based on human rights would thereby be legitimated and empowered to control societal development. The increasingly interventionist state and the growth of corporatism could not dull Durkheim's optimism that increments of individualization and individualism would be a natural, necessary and effective counterbalance to the process of societalization in which central regulation of most spheres of life would replace formerly local and particularistic ways of living. He expected that transformations in religion would therefore ease the process of societalization.

It was left to Durkheim's successors to work out in greater detail the implications for religion of his distinctive understanding of industrial society. Ironically, attention has been focused most intensely on the supposedly pathological features of industrial society and, in particular, on the related notions of anomie and unregulated differentiation. That is, the rapid, but uneven, advances towards specialization and autonomy in different social sectors were held responsible for a state of society marked by a lack of overall regulation and integration. The special significance of religion in industrial society was therefore located in (1) its own progressive separation from other social institutions and (2) the increasing likelihood that individual people would fail to experience a religious sense of belonging to society.

Some responses to the Durkheimian problematic of industrial society took the form of relatively abstract theorizing about the growing importance of functional alternatives to religion in the matter of producing social integration and social system integration (e.g. Davis, 1949; Parsons, 1968).

A second way of applying Durkheim's ideas about industrial society to religion in detail was to study the processes whereby religious groups and other 'intermediary associations' attempted to overcome the problem of anomie. Recognizing that the state had become too remote as a source of moral ideals for ordinary citizens, Durkheim advocated the expansion of middle-range associations in which a sense of solidarity, and hence morality, would be generated. But this strategy has left an abiding ambiguity about the religious claims that might be advanced on behalf of the state in industrial society. It also passed unhelpfully over the fact that social classes and ideological communities would similarly lay claim to moral and/or religious authority independently of both the state and the public realm of civil society. This may be why the Durkheimian perspective has been most assiduously applied to the situation of small minorities and outcast groups (e.g. Poblete, 1960; Plath, 1966).

A third legacy of Durkheim's understanding of industrial society was to direct attention to the process of separation between religion and other social institutions. Differentiation was believed not only to increase the distance between religion and other institutions but also to reduce religion's capacity to function as the 'cement' holding all of a society's institutions together in a cohesive whole. At the same time, the dominance of industrial forms of work organization and the centrality of occupational roles in society were expected to reduce still further the opportunity for religion to exercise a major influence over people's lives (Fenn, 1972). This was the burden of many community studies and of many studies of the growing separation between religion and politics in industrial society. But the full impact of Durkheim's ideas was not felt in the sociology of religion until they had been eagerly, if selectively, assimilated into mid-twentieth-century theories of modernization. These theories placed a one-sided emphasis on religion's integrative capacity and they have subsequently met with strong criticism in the light of religion's growing controversiality.

## RELIGION IN SOCIETY: WEBER

If religion is not regarded as an ideological mystification or a functionally necessary means of generating ideas about the very possibility of society, a different range of sociological problems concerning religion comes into focus. In particular, severing the close connections made by Durkheim between religion and its allegedly societal origins and constant point of reference has the effect of constituting religion as something potentially other than, or outside, society. This approach identifies religion as a realm or sphere independent from other social activities – often as a transcendent point of reference over and above the world of purely human activity. The analytical separation of religion from the rest of social life turns the sociological problem of religion into the question of its relationship with 'the world'. The otherwise opposed views of Hegel and Marx are in formal agreement on this point. In broad terms, religion may be invoked to explain two basic processes: legitimation and challenge.

In other words, religion may be said to have the effect of either justifying certain features of the world or criticizing them. It should be added, of course, that the adoption of this particular sociological perspective does not imply any necessary commitment to belief in the reality of transcendent entities. The emphasis is firmly on the social conditions and *effects* of such beliefs – regardless of their truth.

In different ways, the relationship between religion and the human world has been the focus of many sociological studies of religion, but the work of Max Weber and Ernst Troeltsch has been virtually paradigmatic for the sociology of religion in Western countries. The differences between Weber and his erstwhile student, Troeltsch, are important from some points of view [4] but have little bearing on my general argument about their shared tendency to assume that religion and the world can be separated for analytical purposes. The first assumption underlying their work is that the relationship between religion and society is contingent and variable. The second assumption is that it makes no sense to think in terms of religion in general: the religion/society relationship can only be examined in its historical and socio-cultural specificity. The third assumption is that the relationship tends to develop in a determinate direction.

These three assumptions plainly underlie Weber's series of studies of the potential that is contained in various religions for the rationalization of social processes, social structures and culture. The capacity for instrumental rationality in Ancient Judaism, Islam, Hinduism, Buddhism, Confucianism and Taoism, in comparison with that of the Christian, and specifically Protestant, religion is shown to have been differentially affected by contingent social factors. The rationalization of the modern industrial world, however, is shown to have been greatly (and paradoxically) aided by certain features of Protestantism and of the contingent structural features of post-Reformation Europe. Weber traced the dominant traits of Western modernity back to their unlikely historical and socio-cultural origins in Ancient Judaism, whilst implying that the continuing dominance of non-rational tradition in other parts of the world follows from their lack of a similar conjunction of religious and social factors. The trend towards rationalization, once identified, helped Weber to explain further aspects of the religion/society relationship in the West but without contradicting the first assumption about contingency.

The whole exercise is premissed on an implicit distinction, for analytical purposes, between religion and the world. The two are nevertheless shown to affect each other in certain circumstances, and the outcome is said to be formative for historical trends – including the subsequent capacity of religion to impinge on human affairs. It is not surprising, then, that a tone of irony pervades so many of Weber's writings on religion and society.

The analytic distance between religion and society was maintained by Weber in his studies of general social processes and structures. For example, the legitimation of patterned inequalities in life-chances or authority is crucial to his understanding of the process of transition from tradition to modernity. Religion, as a separate point of transcendental reference outside society, is therefore regarded as a powerful source of ideas and sentiments which could be used to justify the prevailing patterns. This is why Weber thought it necessary to investigate theodicies and the religious legitimations of social arrangements. In this way, he was able to represent many areas of social life as fields where rival claims to legitimation were fought out in struggles for power between competing interest groups.

By keeping religion and society analytically distinct Weber was able to lay the foundations for a distinctive approach to secularization. It turns on the belief that the distance between the spheres of religion and society has been steadily reduced to the point where religion can no longer serve as either an effective legitimator of, or a challenger to, the world. Instead, both are subject to so much rationalization that religion loses its power to legitimize or challenge; and society's basic processes can proceed on the basis of a strictly functional rationality requiring no transcendental warrant.

It is against the background of these arguments about the progressive loss of separation between religion and the world that Weber's fascination with sectarian types of religiosity takes on special significance. The sect-type of religious collectivity stood for social exclusiveness, doctrinal purity and rigorous ethical consistency. The church-type, by contrast, stood for social inclusiveness, doctrinal latitude and a degree of ethical relativism. In other words, the sect-type tried consistently to maintain distance from the world, whereas the church-type sought to influence the world from within. The conceptual distinction helped to account for the typical fortunes of religious groups in the modern world, that is, either purity in marginality or compromise in power (Yinger, 1946).

The conceptual opposition between church and sect arises, then, from the different ways in which they mediate the relationship between religion and the world. This sets the scene for a major historical scenario in which both types are shown ironically to have contributed to their own corruption. The sect promotes a form of disciplined social activity which, despite its non-worldly orientation, incidentally tends to bring about relative success in scientific and practical matters. The unsought prosperity or power of sectarians is believed to jeopardize their highly principled indifference to material things. On a more general plane, Weber argued that sectarian ethics have inspired cultural change outside the ranks of sect members. Many of the moral and attitudinal prerequisites of scientific objectivity, technological ambition, tolerance and moral consistency are traced back to sectarian origins. 'The world' therefore triumphs over pure spirit.

The world triumphs over spirit in the church-type for different reasons. Its social inclusiveness, real or sought after, and its aspiration to be relevant to all aspects of life and all sections of society are said to be congruent with a social ethic which places a high value on harmony and accommodation. Adjustment to prevailing social arrangements is encouraged, and relatively little encouragement is given to spiritual virtuosity among the laity. Priests and religious are subject to a more demanding ethic, and their charisma of office discourages them from full participation in the economic or political realm. The result is that the church-type achieves considerable stability, continuity and influence – but on condition of becoming a formalized and rationalized kind of organization which aspires to legitimate and exclusive control over religious matters. It therefore seeks to make membership *compulsory*, and this further reduces the distance between religion and the world.

The disenchantment of the world, the calculability of everything, was more of a tendency than an accomplished fact in Weber's opinion. He believed that the search for value, meaning and direction in life would continue to be conducted at the level of the individual person, although he conceded that the social setting for this personal search was often small fellowships. Indeed, Weber interpreted many of the changes that were taking place in the Christian churches of his day as evidence that a more personal and private type of spirituality was being cultivated alongside the progressive rationalization of other spheres of life. The ideal of spiritual autonomy therefore accompanied the facts of growing impersonality, bureaucratization and central control in Western states. In this way the boundary between religion and the world was maintained, although its socio-cultural location was shifting. Religion was becoming a personal and private affair, increasingly divorced from the affairs of the disenchanted public realm.

### RELIGION AND SOCIAL ETHICS: TROELTSCH

The idea that the socio-cultural roots of modern Western rationality could be found in the asceticism of Protestant sects was shared by Weber's student, Ernst Troeltsch. There are other continuities between their work, but their conclusions about the likely fate of Christian institutions were notably divergent. Whereas Weber believed that only sporadic outbursts of charismatic leadership would challenge the progressive institutionalization of rationality, Troeltsch maintained a stronger conviction that liberal church-type Protestantism could continue to exercise some influence over the direction of social change. This conviction arose from his magisterial survey of the complex dynamics between the three primary forms of collectivity in which Christian teachings had been embodied: church, sect and mysticism.[5] Each type represented an outworking of selected New Testament ideas and values in application to everyday life. In other words, Troeltsch's project was to understand the trajectory of three broad types of social ethics – each springing from New Testament sources. The project clearly presupposed, then, the kind of analytic distinction between religion and 'the world' that Weber had also employed.[6] But the reason for making the distinction was that it would supposedly help to explain the variety of ways in which Christian social ethics had acted on the world and had themselves been shaped in the process.

Troeltsch regarded the church-type as historically and theologically normative because of its claim objectively to embody spiritual powers and to dispense them universally by means of sacraments. The would-be universalist church-type is poorly placed to resist the tendency to adapt and accommodate itself to prevailing social conditions but it is strongly placed to influence the course of events. By contrast, the sect-type aspires to preserve the purity of its doctrines and practices by excluding people who are spiritually or morally unqualified. It therefore forgoes the chance of directly influencing affairs outside its own usually sharply demarcated boundaries and is consequently not drawn into compromises with prevailing values, ideas, or material interests. The third social expression of Christianity, mysticism, aspires to honour the ideal of culti-vating inward spiritual perfection in individuals by eschewing concerns with supposedly objective expressions of truth or would-be pure fellowships of uniquely qualified religionists.

According to Troeltsch each social 'carrier' of Christianity occupies a distinctive location in society; and each cultivates a distinctive type of social ethics. The church-type, with its teachings of Relative Natural Law and objectified Grace, accepts the frailties and failings of human beings *sub specie aeternitatas*. It therefore encourages a cautiously positive atti-tude towards mundane affairs, modifying its position in the light of experience but always offering forgiveness for sins. By contrast, the sect-type insists on standards of ethical conduct which are rigorous and rigorously consistent with scriptural injunctions. The purity of the sectarian fellowship cannot tolerate major ethical inconsistencies. Instead, it requires disciplined obedience to all ethical precepts, and it can punish transgressors by the ultimate sanction of exclusion from 'the company of the saints'. In comparison, the social ethics of mysticism are much less clear and certainly less formalized. They appear to be confined to virtues such as tolerance, compassion and authenticity. Lacking objective embodiments of sacred power and a socially exclusive kind of fellowship, mysticism is content for compatible sentiments and dispositions to develop spontaneously from the sacredness inherent in every human individual.

Troeltsch employed this threefold typology in order to explain the changing pattern of the Christian religion's interplay with, and distance from, the affairs of the world. He was therefore able to show that a particular configuration of emphases among the three basic types can be detected at any point in history and that they exist in a dynamic tension with each other. This ensures continual change in the actual location of Christianity in society, although Roman Catholicism in the thirteenth century and Protestantism in some countries in the seventeenth century were both regarded as relatively stable syntheses because they enabled principles derived from church-type social ethics to draw together many aspects of culture and society. But Troeltsch despaired of perceiving any clear or orderly patterns in the relations between religion, social ethics and social action in the early twentieth century. If Christianity were still capable of influencing the world, he argued, it would be only by *indirect* means and with occasionally ironic results. Neither church-type, sect-type, nor mysticism was an appropriate organizational vehicle of modern Christianity, but Troeltsch supported the idea of a loosely organized ecumenical grouping of different Christian bodies. On the question of precisely how Christianity would influence the modern world Troeltsch maintained a virtual silence. He only insisted that the outcome would depend at least as much on economic and political circumstances as on religious ideas. He did not appear to think it likely that any great religious figures would emerge in modernity to impose a new version of Christianity on any important sections of society.

For Troeltsch, then, the problem of religion in modernity was an ironic consequence of its very success in earlier periods of history when the effect of some radical Christian ideas on certain societies in Europe and North America had been to create the conditions in which notions of tolerance, compassion, discipline and rationality were able to develop in independence from their religious origins. It was by means of these ideas that Christianity and the world came to terms with each other, but the success of the arrangement tended to deprive Christian churches of a truly external and privileged position from which to continue the critical moulding of social developments. Moreover, political and economic institutions progressively freed themselves from directly religious control, and nation-states came to perceive their own interests as being separable from those of any particular religious organization. The significance of religion in the modern world therefore seemed to be restricted to the fact that it could still contribute partially towards the definition of values, on the basis of which choices could be made by individuals or collectivities between competing goals and strategies. But in this respect religious ideas, which had already been weakened by the European Enlightenment and by Pietism, were in an unequal competition with powerful material and scientific interests which were largely indifferent to religious considerations. The open question in Troeltsch's mind in the first two decades of the twentieth century was whether future economic and political conjunctures would ever make it possible for Christian ideas to regain a decisive influence on events in the world. His faith in the eternal value of the Christian religion appeared to be undiminished by his honest admission that he could not foresee how Christianity could be restored to a position of sociological importance.

In short, the most important thing about religion for both Weber and Troeltsch was that it is, by definition, separate from the world but, by necessity, increasingly compromised with it. The underlying process is therefore one of entropy, corruption and 'disenchantment'. The primary significance of the transition to industrial society is that it boosted this process in general but that, in addition, it ironically gave rise to fleeting moments of resistance and rebellion.

One of the principal legacies from Weber and Troeltsch was a set of interpretive categories which emphasized the gradual ascendancy of intellectualized and calculative reason over the values which had traditionally given meaning to human affairs in Western societies. This process of rationalization was regarded as a prime determinant of the modern Western world and the chief agent of religion's decline. The loss or corruption of the formerly autonomous sphere of values (transcendent and otherwise) was believed to herald the 'polar night of icy darkness' and the 'disenchantment of the world'. The application of standards of instrumental rationality to everything would therefore result in an irrational world completely lacking in any meaning beyond its own procedural regularity and efficiency. But rationalization was neither inevitable nor uniform in its progress and effects.

This particular scenario for industrial society, or the 'modern rational world' in Weber's preferred terms, depicts religion as a progressively marginalized, intellectualized and bureaucratized phenomenon (Harrison, 1959) with consequently declining capacity to exert any independent influence over the actions of individuals or collectivities. In particular, actions which were formerly the means to attaining religious values are transformed into ends in themselves, thereby dispensing with a transcendental point of reference (Zald, 1970).

Although rationalization was expected to diminish the overall social force of religion, there was still an interest in the separate fates of the different types of religious collectivity. In fact, the belief that religious values (and all other substantive values) were vulnerable to the corrupting power of 'the world' helped Weber and Troeltsch to set up the ideal-typical distinction between church and sect. A zero-sum relationship between transcendental purity and worldly compromise was posited as the basis for the sect-like and church-like configurations of ethics, doctrine and social relationships. Numerous variants of this religious and moral economy have been subsequently devised to account for the dynamics of Christian organizations in industrial society (Yinger, 1946; Pfautz, 1956). A further embellishment of the theme of the religio-moral economy of church-type and sect-type was associated with Weber's notion that charisma had the power to overturn institutionalized forms of religion from time to time before itself becoming institutionalized in new forms (Wilson, 1975). But there are enough ambiguities in Weber's writings to permit speculation about the possibility that charisma might continue to interrupt the modern world's order (Séguy, 1985).

CONCLUSION

Marx, Durkheim, Weber and Troeltsch may have been agreed on the basic point that industrializing societies were undergoing massive transformations, but the meanings that each of them attributed to the transformations were widely different in key respects. None of them attributed primary significance, for example, to the 'industrial' character of the dominant mode of production. Yet they all regarded it in their different ways as an important symptom of the forces that were considered to be the real determinants of social change – contradictions between the forces and social relations of production; the rapid advance of the division of labour in society; and the process of rationalization. Their understandings of the role of religion in the emergent industrial societies showed no less variety. Moreover, their interpretations of religion were eventually to have a formative influence on sociologists' thinking about religion in the vastly changed circumstances of the mid-twentieth century.

It would be a mistake, however, to assume that Marx, Durkheim, Weber and Troeltsch provided 'theories' of industrial society with a determinate place for religion. On the contrary, they provided extensive analysis of the past and of the transformations through which their societies were passing. There were also broad intimations of the future direction of social change, but it was the character of the changes which received the most attention: not an underlying theory of change. This accords with C. Wright Mills's

(1959) assessment of the 'classic tradition' in sociology: it is characterized by the generally broad questions that it raised about transformations in whole societies and about the role of individual humans within these transformations. As a consequence of this piecemeal approach to sociology, the phenomenon of religion was investigated almost entirely in terms of its implications for relatively specific aspects of change. Religion was not, with the possible exception of Marx's early work, examined in relation to a rounded model of industrial society. It was Talcott Parsons and some of his collaborators, as we shall see in Chapter 3, who eventually accomplished this task.

## NOTES

1 See Turner, 1983, for the ambiguities concealed in this formulation.

2 It has also given rise to an inconclusive debate about the degree of relative autonomy between the 'base' and the 'superstructure'.

3 But it must be admitted that Durkheim's vision of the whole world as a totality eventually welded together by an ethos of individualism and universal fraternity smacks more of utopianism than of the cold-blooded positivism of which he is so frequently and wrongly accused.

4 See, for example, Eister, 1973, and Beckford, 1975.

5 Steeman, 1984, argued that Troeltsch also identified the Free Church as a fourth type akin to what is nowadays called 'the denomination'.

6 'Le problème de Troeltsch est celui du rapport entre croyance chrétienne et monde profane. Quelle influence excercent-ils l'un sur l'autre?' (Séguy, 1980, p. 257).

# 3

# Fallow period and second harvest

## FROM GOLDEN AGE TO FALLOW PERIOD IN EUROPE

There is a tendency in some quarters to regard the late nineteenth and early twentieth centuries as a 'golden age' for the sociology of religion. The concept of 'the sacred' has even been described as the key to the unique role played by sociology in this period. Bryan Wilson's opinion, for example, is that religion is 'a subject at the heart of classical sociological theory, and it remains true today that it continues to be at the core of the discipline' (1982, p. 9).

I would like to make two critical comments on this idea. First, it overlooks the fact that, in their different ways, each of the 'golden age' sociologists accounted primarily for the *decline* of religion as a social force. It is as if the initial success of the sociology of religion had been achieved only by constituting religion as a social phenomenon which supposedly had no future. Religion served as a convenient subject for scholars wanting to demonstrate sociology's capacity to explain, or to explain away, the changes which were believed to be essential for the emergence of a new type of society – industrial society. It is no accident, therefore, that the 'golden age' of the sociology of religion apparently coincided with the formative stage of sociological theorizing about industrial society. The decline of religion's social significance was gradually taken to be an essential feature of the industrialization process.

Secondly, with the partial exception of Durkheim's work, very few of the sociological writings which have subsequently been incorporated into the 'classics' were directly concerned with *contemporary* religion. Even fewer made a significant impact on the conduct of sociological research on religion in the first four decades of the twentieth century. Delays in having key works translated into English ensured that Marx's early writings and most of Weber's and Troeltsch's *oeuvre* remained largely unknown beyond the communities of German-speaking scholars before the 1940s. Consequently, their present-day status as classics is based on judgements made about their value many years after their first appearance and, ironically, at a time when their depictions of industrial or capitalist society were already in tension with the realities of mature industrial society.

In other words, the claim that the modern sociology of religion is deeply rooted in classical problematics is complicated by the fact that it is nowadays very difficult to separate the ideas of Marx, Durkheim, Weber and Troeltsch from the theories of industrial or capitalist society which have developed in the intervening period. On the other hand, it is clear that the classics of sociology have been assimilated into various synthetic theories of industrial society in such a way that the classics' separate identities have thereby been downgraded for the sake of an allegedly more inclusive perspective. It is questionable, therefore, whether the continuity between the classics of sociology and the modern sociology of religion is really as strong as has been claimed. The relationship between them is, as will be argued in this and the next chapters, heavily mediated by synthetic theories of industrial society.

It could also be argued that the very insistence on the functional indispensability of religion, which was characteristic of many social theorists in the nineteenth century, helped to deter scholars from undertaking empirical studies of religious phenomena. If the most important feature of religion was its indispensability or universality, there could be few reasons for studying its social forms in detail. A similar conclusion could also have emerged from the Marxian line of reasoning about religion's anticipated demise.

Durkheim's legacy is rather different. Not only were his major writings on religion translated into English and other languages soon after their first publication, but his 'disciples' also actively promoted his ideas long after his death. In fact, the Durkheimian school was the dominant force in French-language anthropology and sociology until the 1960s. Yet, surprisingly few attempts were made to apply Durkheim's ideas to the understanding of religion in contemporary Western societies. As Tiryakian (1981, p. 119) observed: 'ironically, [*The Elementary Forms of the Religious Life*] suffered a period of relative benign neglect by the American sociological profession which lasted until well after the Second World War. Yet it was of great importance to social anthropology'. The French tradition of 'religious sociology' inspired by Le Bras and Boulard, for example, drew very little on Durkheim's ideas in its attempts to explain either the overall decline of Catholic religious practice in France or the regional and occupational variations in levels of practice. It was not until the 1950s, according to Danièle Hervieu-Léger (1986), that the question of 'religious loss' was seriously linked by French sociologists to new questions about modernity and the special dynamics of industrial societies. But even then, the factor which appeared to explain most of the variation in levels of practice was the non-Durkheimian one of the manner in which Christianity had originally been implanted and cultivated not only in regions but also in particular towns and subsections of towns (Boulard and Rémy, 1968).

French sociologists have shown a greater readiness to adopt a Durkheimian perspective on relatively simple, non-industrial societies. To a large extent, Durkheim's contemporaries and immediate successors working in English and French were also more concerned with 'primitive' than with 'modern' religion. The curious reluctance of early Durkheimians to study religion in their own societies is understandable when it is borne in mind that Durkheim had assigned no special privileges, priority or importance to religion as such: only to the integrative and harmonizing *functions* that it happened to perform in non-industrial societies but which could presumably be fulfilled by different agents in industrial societies. It should also be noted here, in anticipation of an argument which will be developed below, that the most innovative proponents of a Durkheimian sociology of religion in the heyday of theorizing about industrial society tended to stress the *obstacles* facing religion in the modern world. Thus, Guy Swanson, Mary Douglas and Claude Lévi-Strauss, for example, have argued in their different ways that the putative 'need' for a religious mode of social integration and social system integration is either outdated, exaggerated, or misconceived.

In short, the era of the sociological classics was followed by a fallow period in which very few notable attempts were made to apply the earlier wisdom, in so far as it was even known, to the study of contemporary religion. In fact, the very idea of taking religious phenomena as a suitable, not to say important, topic for social scientific analysis was slow to develop and actually met with resistance in many places.

Indeed, it would be a mistake to believe that the various classical contributions to the sociology of religion went unchallenged even in their own day. For all the acclaim that Comte and Saint-Simon, for example, won as the founders of the subject, it should not be forgotten that in their own day their ideas had been in conflict with a long tradition of more conservative thinking, according to which religious institutions represented the quintessence of civilized culture. For example, Edmund Burke, Louis Bonald and Joseph de Maistre each saw great sociological significance in religion without sharing the Positivists' ironic conviction that, aside from its latent function of generating societal stability, religion was doomed to be supplanted by the growing power of science. Indeed, the predominantly rationalistic tendency of the sociological classics was continuously criticized and disparaged by the no less sociological ideas of numerous conservative thinkers throughout the nineteenth century. The extensive contributions of Le Play and the French 'Social Catholics' actually laid the foundations for a sociology of industrial society which totally rejected the secular rationalism of some of their contemporaries who went on to become much better known as the founders of sociology.

There is a good reason, then, for drawing attention to the interval that separated the classical works of sociology from their widespread application in the study of religion. For, leaving aside the immediate take-up of Durkheim's ideas about religion in pre-industrial societies, it was not until the late 1930s that the thinking of Marx, Durkheim and Weber was integrated into general theories of industrial or capitalist society by English-speaking sociologists. In other words, although discussions of religion played a prominent part in the classics of early sociology, the light that was cast on religion as such was not the feature which most impressed their successors. The classics were appreciated for their synoptic visions of the broad changes that could then be seen to have either preceded or accompanied the transition from pre-industrial to industrial society. They were found to convey powerful images of the driving forces of change and their effects on a wide range of social institutions, structures and practices. Their treatment of religion could not be separated from the wider 'landscapes' of social change which were attributed to them.

To be more specific, de Tocqueville was probably the only member of the founding generation of sociologists to take the trouble to analyse in detail the religious affairs of his day. Comte, Saint-Simon, Spencer, Marx, Engels, Durkheim, Weber and Simmel preferred, instead, to study at best the implications that they foresaw for religion in the master trends of social change. In some cases, there was also a keen interest in the historical transformations of religious ideas, practices and organizations in so far as they were believed to *illustrate* the force and direction of supposedly underlying cultural or societal tendencies. This is particularly evident in the strongly evolutionist and intellectualist leanings of the leaders of British anthropology from the late nineteenth century until the Second World War. Both Herbert Spencer and Edmund Tylor, for example, subscribed to the idea that the religions of primitive people represented a faulty kind of rationality which was destined to be superseded, as in industrializing countries, by soundly based scientific knowledge. F. Max Müller's theory that the attribution of special powers to natural phenomena involved a linguistic error at least had the virtue of being based on extensive comparative scholarship but it also shared the contemporary fixation with cognitive matters. Similarly, J. G. Frazer's intuition that religion was an outgrowth from magic and that the latter originated in faulty reasoning by analogy reinforced the intellectualist tendency to dispose of religion as defective science. Only W. Robertson Smith and R. R. Marrett stand out as a source of insights into the ritual and symbolic, rather than narrowly cognitive, aspects of religion. This line of approach was strengthened in the 1920s by B. Malinowski's rejection of evolutionism.

The lack of informed interest in religious phenomena was particularly marked among the founding generation of sociologists in Edwardian Britain. Their overriding preoccupation with political economy and with questions about the structure of opportunities for education and social mobility left little room for the consideration of religion in their own society. In any case, the prevailing rationalism, empiricism and evolutionism did not cast religion in an interesting or even challenging light – except in so far as its prominent place in pre-industrial societies could be profitably contrasted with its diminished importance in industrial societies. This is clearly illustrated by, for example, Westermaarck's *The Origin and Development of Moral Ideas* (1906), Hobhouse's *Morals in Evolution* (1906) and Hobhouse, Wheeler and Ginsberg's *The Material Culture and Social Institutions of the Simpler Peoples* (1915). Another reason for the relative lack of interest in the sociology of contemporary religion in Britain was the belief that sociology, especially in the shape of eugenics, represented a new form of religion in itself.

The situation was rather different in Germany, although the practice of ignoring or avoiding sociological study of contemporary religion in the inter-war years was maintained. The difference arose from the fact that, in the tradition of the *Geisteswissenschaften* and under the influence of *die verstehende Soziologie*, German scholars were drawn towards the construction of historically based typologies of social and cultural phenomena. Debates about the contribution of religious forces to the development of various types of capitalism, rationality and social ethics, for example, were in the forefront of the nascent social sciences. They had the effect of focusing the interests of historians, economists, jurists, philosophers and sociologists on common problems, and of thereby integrating the understanding of religion into the mainstream of academic life. As a result, religion was considered interesting not solely in pre-industrial societies or exclusively in terms of its integrative functions. It was regarded as a crucial facet of the evolving distinctiveness of the Western world and, as such, was considered worthy of detailed examination. The preferred approach was principally historical and typological, with considerable scope for phenomenological methods. Leading exponents of this approach included Werner Sombart, Max Weber, Georg Jellinek, Georg Simmel, Ernst Troeltsch and Joachim Wach.

The fact that the classics of sociology, which are widely believed to have been preoccupied with religion, dealt mainly with religion as an expedient or as a means of illuminating some other contemporary phenomena helps to explain two things. First, it throws some light on the question of why sociological studies of early-twentieth-century religion in industrializing countries were few in number and relatively indifferent to the approaches that had been adopted by the classical authors. It also helps to explain why, according to Birnbaum (1956), it is paradoxical that the sociology of religion appeared to be so weak by the mid-twentieth century in Britain where so many notable contributions to the subject had been written in the previous century.

Secondly, it makes it easier to understand why the sociology of religion which began to flourish in the mid-twentieth century mainly pursued a limited range of topics which were largely determined by the ways in which the classics had been assimilated into synthetic, all-purpose theories of industrial society. That is, preoccupations with the major themes of secularization and church/sect dynamics are an out-working of the triumphalist philosophies of history which pervaded mid-twentieth-century understanding of industrial society.

Yet, the predominance of evolutionary perspectives of widely varying kinds should not blind us to the fact that, for all their emphasis on change and adaptation, the classical sociologists and their immediate successors tended to operate with *static* conceptions of religion. Indeed, it suited their diverse purposes to be able to contrast the assumed time-lessness of religion with the forces of change in industrializing societies. It was also useful from their point of view to be able to make a contrast between the attachment of major religious organizations to tradition and the assumed readiness of secular organizations to adapt to changes in their environment. The oppositions between the categories of sacred and profane or religious and secular were central to the logics of evolutionary thinking. The presumed dynamics of societies as social systems determined the expected decline of religion. The legacy of these contrasts can be seen quite clearly in, for example, Howard S. Becker's explicit association of the sacred with resistance to change (Becker, 1957). Secularity was therefore defined in terms of openness to change. There is an even stronger echo of this association between religion and conservation in Talcott Parsons's views on religion, as we shall see below. It was only in the 1960s that sociologists began to voice the objection that the actual conservatism and relatively static character of the main Christian churches in the later Middle Ages gave no clue to the essential nature or functions of religion. Acquaviva (1966) developed this line of reasoning on the grounds that the human experience of the sacred was separable from its cultural forms of expression in time and space, whereas Bellah (1970) preferred to deny the inevitability of secularization on the grounds of a human need for symbols of ultimate meaning.

### A FRESH START IN THE UNITED STATES

The impact of classical sociology on studies of religion in Western Europe before the 1940s was, as we indicated above, remarkably weak. The situation in the USA was scarcely different, but the reasons for the fallow period were different in several important respects. For, in addition to the lack of translations into English of many key works, there were institutional. factors which cast the problem of religion in a distinctively American light.

In the first place, the rate of participation in organized religion was still increasing in the urban areas of the USA in the first half of the twentieth century. Religion, in its mainly Protestant guise, was a prominent and growing feature of public life; and it met with *relatively* little opposition from organized scepticism, anti-clericalism, or atheism. Moreover, the influx of migrants from countries in which Judaism and Roman Catholicism in particular were still powerful swelled the ranks of religionists especially in urban centres. Religious organizations acted both as reception centres for successive waves of new immigrants and as channels of integration into public life. There is a loud echo of this in the subsequent preoccupation of US sociologists with the integrative potential of religion.

Secondly, although (or, perhaps, because) the First Amendment to the Federal Constitution explicitly prohibited the entanglement of the state in any matters of religion, religious organizations were among the most prominent and active participants in public life. Religious organizations were particularly prominent, for example, in schemes to moderate the worst excesses of chaotic and rapid development in the cities of the eastern seaboard and the north-eastern states.

Thirdly, sociology found a place in the syllabus of many institutions of higher education far more readily than was possible in the early twentieth century in Europe. Many of these institutions were either religious foundations or colleges with an express commitment to the practical improvement of the material and moral conditions of life. The result was that sociology came to be widely regarded as a contribution towards the progressive construction of the USA. This effect was heightened in the aftermath of the Civil War and in the midst of hectic immigration and westwards migration in the closing decades of the nineteenth century. Thus: 'Because religion for them was an inspirational *resource*, the first American sociologists, unlike their contemporaries in Europe, did not regard spiritual guidance or theodicy . . . as topics for investigation' (Vidich and Lyman, 1985, p. 1). The fact that religion was more of a resource than a topic for sociology has been confirmed by research into the treatment of religion in the main US journals of sociology between 1895 and 1929. Opinions are divided on this issue, but the majority view is that the sociology of religion was dominated by committed religionists and that their major concern was with Social Gospel issues (Reed, 1981; but see also Swatos, 1984).

The combination of these three institutional facts helps to explain the distinctive character of some of the earliest problematics to dominate sociology in the USA. For, even in the case of those European classics (for example, Comte and Spencer) which were widely discussed among US intellectuals at the turn of the nineteenth and twentieth centuries there was a strong tendency to filter out the anti-religious and cynical elements in favour of a meliorist interpretation of sociology's value. A strong affinity has, in fact, been widely observed between three things: Puritan concerns with human beings' collective stewardship of God's earth; the Social Gospel's contribution towards social engineering; and positivism's faith in the capacity of scientific knowledge, correctly applied, to solve all of society's major problems. Even the least religiously minded of the first generation of US sociologists, Lester Ward, had faith in the power of human reason to generate the kind of practical understanding of human affairs which would help to solve the outstanding social problems of the USA in the early stages of industrialization and urbanization, in particular the glaring inequalities of class, gender and race. Ward expected religion to fade away into relative insignificance in the face of the evident successes of positivistic and evolutionary science. He regarded the future of industrial society as likely to be all the more harmonious and prosperous for the replacement of religion by science.

W. G. Sumner had very different reasons for being sceptical about the value of religion in the future of US society. Rejecting the contemporary fashion for positivism, rationalism and evolutionism he nevertheless believed that a new moral order based on the values of competitive individualism within a political order governed by *laissez-faire* principles might be able to emerge in time. There was no point in trying to bolster or revive the former prestige of Puritan values, but, according to Sumner, there was everything to be said for encouraging the crystallization of new values associated with the individualistic struggle for success within the framework of capitalism and independently of state welfarism. Religious institutions were regarded as relevant only to the extent that they could adapt to the newly competitive circumstances. Otherwise, they were allegedly doomed to irrelevance. These ideas did not make Sumner popular with the religious authorities of Yale College, and his early career as an Episcopal clergyman was not sufficient evidence, in the eyes of his critics, of his continuing commitment to the gospel of Christianity. In fact, it is difficult to detect any specifically Christian elements in his mature works.

By contrast, as is better known, Albion Small's commitment to Christianity never wavered, although his early conviction that sociology could serve as a vehicle for Christianizing US society was eventually abandoned. He saw no necessity for conflict between science and Christianity, believing, instead, that they both represented a search for higher meaning in different but compatible realms of reality. His belief was that the promotion of science would help to diffuse a 'Christian spirit' through industrial society, thereby prefiguring A. E. Ross's view that the task of social reform was too great for the Christian churches and should be taken up by sociology. This was a recurrent theme of articles in the *American Journal of Sociology* under Small's editorship and is further evidence of the essentially practical and humanitarian orientation of US sociology in its formative period. Christianity was incorporated for the humanitarian values with which it could be associated: not for its theological or devotional aspects.

It was at Harvard University, however, that probably the most formative influence on US sociology's understanding of the place of religion in the emerging industrial order was registered. Significantly, the most lasting impressions were made by scholars whose commitment to Protestant versions of Christianity ensured that the sociology of industrial society would not neglect religion. The range of contributions was broad, however, and included the ethically based urban planning of F. G. Peabody, the eugenic Social Gospel of Edward Cummings, the optimistic evolutionism of Thomas Nixon Carver and the managerial psychology of Hugo Munsterberg. The overall effect of their separate contributions has been described, with some exaggeration, as a transvaluation of the Puritan notion of a covenant between God and the elect:

Harvard's thinkers approached the problem of reconstituting the covenant from two directions. Individual salvation could be achieved by restoring the soul (mind, psyche) of the individual; anyone who accepted society's core values could experience a secular version of rebirth. Societal salvation could be achieved by developing sociopsychological technologies for the administration of industry and business and for spreading and indoctrinating everyone with the values necessary to sustain overall harmony in America. In the spirit of a democratic ethos, all were eligible for participation in the new industrial order of society.

(Vidich and Lyman, 1985, p. 98)

Other formative influences on US sociology's dominant ways of grasping the nature of early-twentieth-century society included Franklin H. Giddings's belief, which was shared and developed by his associates and students at Columbia University, that the social form of Protestant denominations had already established the mould for all manner of voluntary associations and that they, in turn, were to ensure the orderly growth of a harmonious public life in the USA's increasingly heterogeneous and rapidly changing society. The social survey and methods of statistical analysis were developed to assess the extent to which harmony and consensus were actually being produced and, thereby, to provide the empirical basis for a comparative study of societies in terms of their progress towards 'civilized' values. Social statistics were also considered essential for social engineering, and this theme was energetically advocated by Albion Small at the University of Chicago and by others at several other midwestern universities.

The distinctive combination of intellectual, religious, moral and practical influences on the shaping of sociology in the USA at the beginning of the twentieth century paved the way for an equally distinctive set of problematics concerning the place of religion in the prevailing concepts of industrial society. In the thinking of even the least religious sociologists, the European practice of opposing the sacred and the secular enjoyed very little favour. The conceptual distinction between religion and 'the world' also carried little weight, and the idea that religion might actually cease to exist in a classless society remained highly implausible if not unthinkable. On the other hand, it must be added that there was a tendency to conceive of religion in largely functionalist terms as a repository of ultimate values and meanings rather than as a distinctive set of beliefs, sentiments and practices. Contrary to popular belief, the earliest US sociologists were not particularly devout or pious Christians (Leuba, 1916; Swatos, 1984). Many of them favoured a liberal and humanitarian respect for the utility of broadly Christian values in the task of social reform. Others regarded Christian values as key resources in the struggle for survival and power among individuals and social classes. But questions of theology, ecclesiology and liturgy were of little interest to the founding generation of US sociologists. Indeed, the significance of specifically Christian beliefs and organizations was generally downplayed in favour of self-consciously scientific or technocratic approaches to the understanding and solution of social problems.

Exceptions must be made, however, for a small number of scholars who remained sceptical about the direction in which the mainstream of US sociology was heading. In particular, H. Richard Niebuhr (1929) remained firmly committed to his view that Christian religious organizations were

> sociological groups whose principle of differentiation is to be sought in their conformity to the order of social classes and castes. It would not be true to affirm that the denominations are not religious groups with religious purposes, but it is true that they represent the accommodation of religion to the caste system . . . Denominationalism thus represents the moral failure of Christianity.
>
> (1929, p. 25)

Here, the emphasis was firmly on the social divisions and conflicts of modern society which, with increasing societal differentiation, were expected to undermine the very possibility of a truly Christian civilization. It is highly significant for my argument that Niebuhr's debt to Troeltsch and Weber was considerable and was clearly reflected in Niebuhr's special interest in the appropriateness of the sect-type to disprivileged sections of US society. An optimistic echo of Troeltsch could also be heard in Niebuhr's belief that 'the church of fellowship in love' could one day emerge from the divisive denominational system and create Christian unity. This theme was taken up at greater length in subsequent works, but it was the *Social Sources* which held most relevance to the sociology of religion.

The influence of Niebuhr's robust treatment of the social vehicles of Christianity can also be seen in, for example, Liston Pope's *Millhands and Preachers* (1942) and in J. Milton Yinger's *Religion in the Struggle for Power* (1946). Both of these pioneering studies implicitly agreed that 'Christian ethics will not permit a world-fleeing asceticism which seeks purity at the cost of service. At the end, if not at the beginning of every effort to incorporate Christianity, there is, therefore, a compromise' (Niebuhr, 1929, p. 5). The result was a varied set of ideas about the necessarily fragile and short-lived commitment to doctrinal and social purity in the sect-type. The sect-to-denomination process was therefore located in a fundamental problem of both doctrine and organization, with the notion of *power* being central to the whole dynamic. The religious history of the USA could be interpreted as a struggle for power between the relatively powerful and the relatively deprived sections of society. The element of *Realpolitik* was eventually, as we shall see later in this chapter, replaced by questions about the function of sects as agents of social mobility and of resocialization into dominant values.

Will Herberg's *Protestant-Catholic-Jew* (1955) and Gerhard Lenski's *The Religious Factor* (1961) can be considered as a bridge between a concern with the social divisiveness of religious organizations in the USA and the newly emerging interest in religion as an institution which had the potential to overcome divisiveness and to integrate the whole of an industrial society. But it is worth noting Lenski's belief that 'Less systematic sociological research has been devoted to religion than to any other major institution of our society' (1961, p. 2). This was not an exaggeration, and it accords with my argument that the era of the classics was followed by a lengthy fallow period which came to an end in the 1950s when

Talcott Parsons and other functionalists turned their attention to the capacity of religion to integrate 'modern' industrial (and, by extension, 'modernizing') societies.[1] It is significant for my purposes, however, that Lenski concluded his research with a qualified prediction that the 'compartmentalization' between religious groups was the best that Americans could hope for in this increasingly divided society. His fear was that the ethical and spiritual elements of religion would be overwhelmed by political considerations if religious groups became more compartmentalized. This fear was to be echoed in some of Robert Bellah's work and was to be confirmed by the recrudescence of church/state problems in the 1970s.

## A SECOND FRESH START IN AMERICA

Although Talcott Parsons acknowledged very few debts to early US sociologists, their tendency to accentuate the general importance of Christian values blossomed in his theories of modernization and industrial society as well as in the work of numerous other US sociologists who were strongly influenced by him. But it must be added that Parsons's early preoccupations with a voluntaristic theory of action and the late flowering of a long-standing interest in continuities between the cybernetic systems of living organisms and human societies are only tangential to the theoretical ideas which conditioned sociological thinking about religion in the USA in the mid-twentieth century. Admittedly, *The Structure of Social Action* (1937) had already synthesized a number of 'classical' theories from sociology and economics into a general social theory in which normative components (values, beliefs and norms) were regarded as both the mainspring and governor of social action, but it was the products of the middle phase of Parsons's career which exercised the greatest influence over the sociology of religion. In particular, *The Social System* (1951) and *Toward a General Theory of Action* (Parsons and Shils, 1951) laid down the framework of concepts which constituted religion as a special part of the system of industrial societies. More specific analyses of religion were also made at this time in such essays as 'The pattern of religious organization in the United

States' (1958) and 'Mental illness and "spiritual malaise": the roles of the psychiatrist and the minister of religion' (1960c).

Religion was also a topic of *methodological* importance for Parsons because it had been reduced to a purely epiphenomenal status by positivists and behaviourists. He argued that Pareto, Malinowski, Durkheim and Weber, by contrast, had each made major contributions towards a more satisfactory way of studying religion. By synthesizing aspects of their widely differing approaches to religion Parsons was able to illustrate the superiority that he claimed for a voluntaristic theory of social action which emphasized the need to take into account (1) the cognitive and evaluative beliefs of actors, (2) the functional contribution of normatively patterned social actions towards the systemic order of society and (3) the importance of values and beliefs as sources of adaptive social change. It therefore suited Parsons's methodological purposes to pay special attention to religion as a topic of sociological analysis; it served him well in the struggle against positivist and behaviourist doctrines of science.

The *substantive* importance of religion for Parsons was, by comparison, much greater. Religion occupied a crucial place in his increasingly complex models of social action and social systems. There are, in fact, good grounds for describing the theoretical orientation of his work from about the 1950s to the mid-1960s as 'normative functionalism'. This label emphasizes Parsons's claim that, in any system of action, the strategic choices are governed by norms and values. Indeed, the stability of institutionalized practices and the degree of consistency between them are regarded as the product of value orientations.

Moreover, the faith that Parsons placed in the benign effects of core values on the continuing prosperity and apparent stability of US society (at least, the white middle-class section) appeared to be validated by the growing strength of religious organizations in the 1950s and 1960s. This period represented a high water mark for liberal denominations and was also the beginning of a surge of popularity in conservative religious groups. It was as if the functionalist theorems were being demonstrated in practice. This coincidence of the functionalist theoretical tenets and the practical achievements of religious organizations gave a fresh impetus to the sociology of religion, as we shall see in more detail below. But it must be pointed out here that the outcome of this historical coincidence was a tendency virtually to equate 'religion' with formal religious organizations (Luckmann, 1967). This tendency was reinforced by the new-found readiness of the major denominations, in common with other organizations, to sponsor market-oriented sociological research. As a result, the full panoply of positivistic research methods was brought to bear on questions which arose from a normative functionalist perspective on churches.

Accepting Durkheim's identification of religion with the moral force which attaches to society's categorial distinction between sacred things and profane things, Parsons defined religious beliefs as 'systems of cognitive orientation relative to problems of meaning . . . acceptance of which is treated as a moral obligation by the actor' (Parsons, 1951, p. 368). There is a strong connection, therefore, between religion and morality in so far as people are expected to treat them both with an attitude of respect in recognition of their derivation from the level of the social totality. This totality is represented by ideas about a supernatural order.

> The supernatural order thus gives cognitive meaning to the moral-evaluative sentiments and norms of an action system, not in the sense that either the sentiments or the cognitive beliefs have causal priority but that they tend to be integrated with one another, and that this integration is importantly related to the stabilization of the system.
>
> (Parsons, 1951, p. 369)

But, the argument continues, no system of values can avoid frustrations and conflicts. Yet, 'there is always a complex variety of mechanisms in the social system which mitigate the severity of these frustrations and conflicts' (Parsons, 1951, p. 371); so Parsons methodically worked out the logically possible ways of achieving mitigation in circumstances in which institutionalized values are either (1) accepted or (2) rejected. Within each of these two possibilities a distinction was also drawn between mitigation in (1) a transcendental sphere or (2) a future state of society. The result can be represented as in Figure 3.1:

TYPE OF ORIENTATION

| | | Transcendental | This-worldly |
|---|---|---|---|
| ORIENTATION INSTITUTIONAL VALUES | Accept | Other-worldly *Ausgleich* | Progressive |
| | Reject | Radical religions of salvation | Revolution |

**Figure 3.1** The mitigation of frustration in the social system.

Parsons claimed that religion not only 'rationalizes' systems of institutionalized values by mitigating discrepancies between expectations and perceived reality but also *constitutes* the value system to varying degrees. This claim was supported by evidence about the 'tendency to pattern-consistency in the cultural tradition as a whole' (1951, p. 378). In other words, the continuity and strength of value patterns were explained in terms of the overarching function of religion as the chief source of meaning in human life.

The patterns were not considered to be immutable, however. The tension between expectations and perceived reality was also said to be felt *within* each type of religious orientation. Thus, a position of radical salvation may be difficult to maintain if it is adopted by large numbers of people and heavily institutionalized. There is a tendency to try to realize religious values by means of success in 'worldly' projects, but this is likely in the long term to undermine the original orientation. This 'paradox of institutionalization' was not, however, the main mechanism of change in religion, according to Parsons.

A much more ambitious theory of religious change appears in Parsons's account of the forces which have allegedly shaped the modern Western world and which have 'eventuated in modern industrialism'. Pride of place was given to religion and ideology which allegedly function as 'mechanisms of value-indoctrination and maintenance' (Parsons, 1960a, p. 155). The relevance of these mechanisms to industrialism was that 'they must somehow reinforce motivation to participate in higher-order, more mobile types of organization than would be the case in a more highly traditionalized and particularized society' (Parsons, 1960a, p. 155). The process of 'Christianizing' society was believed to have begun early in the history of Christianity and to have received a major boost during the Reformation. It involves the three interrelated processes of (1) the extension of Christian values to more and more spheres of life, (2) the internal differentiation of religious organizations as well as their differentiation from the rest of society and (3) the evolutionary upgrading of standards of ethical conduct inside and outside religious organizations. The outcome was not, however, considered to be secularization. This is one of the most controversial aspects of the Parsonian legacy.

Parsons claimed in the late 1950s that, in the USA, 'As far as organization of political authority was concerned, religion ceased to be a subject of "public" concern, and can be relegated to the sphere of private affairs, except for political guardianship of religious freedom' (Parsons, 1960b, p. 296). In denying that this amounted to secularization in the commonly accepted sense of the elimination of 'organized religion from the social scene' (1960b, p. 298) Parsons argued that 'the relations between religion and society' had been reinstitutionalized in such a way as to give religion 'a redefined place in the social scene' (1960b, p. 298). This strategy preserved the integrity of normative functionalism by maintaining that the contribution of religious values to the stability of the US social system had not been usurped or cancelled out. The system, on the contrary, continued to be essentially guided by values which were rooted in religion – as they had been at least since the creation of the independent USA. The constitutional separation of state and religion in no way detracted from this structural arrangement between religion, values and an orderly social system. Nor, more controversially, did the process of institutional differentiation which progressively divided religion from, for example, politics, education, law and medicine allegedly undermine the functions of religion.

The latter proposition follows, almost by definition, from Parsons's stipulation that

> the 'core' function of religion in the social system [is] the regulation of the balance of motivational commitment of the individual to the values of his society – and through these values to his roles in it as compared with alternative considerations concerning his ultimate fate as a knowing, sentient being . . . [I]n the last analysis religion is an individual matter, a concern of the innermost core of the individual's personality for his own identity and commitments.
>
> (Parsons, 1960b, pp. 302-3)

It follows, then, that the strictly *religious* function could hardly ever be dispensed with in an orderly social system. To this is added the claim that US institutions had the opportunity to develop slowly and without sudden or intolerable pressures. This was said to be helped by the facts that 'religious issues were not a proper subject for political action' (1960b, p. 305) under the Federal Constitution and that the diversity of religious groups in the USA militated against the alignment of political, economic and religious divisions (with the exception of Catholicism in the early twentieth century). Parsons therefore concluded that 'The broad pattern of keeping religion out of politics has come to be stably institutionalized in American society' (Parsons, 1960b, p. 306) in contrast to the situation in, for example, the Province of Quebec.

If this seems to be inconsistent with the evident centrality of religious symbols in much of the USA's public and political life, it was left to Robert Bellah to solve the problem by giving a distinctive twist to the old notion of 'civil religion'.

His argument recognized, on the one hand, that 'matters of personal religious beliefs, worship, and association' are private and therefore have no place in the public world of politics but that, on the other, there is a separate sphere of beliefs, symbols and rituals which gives public voice to 'common elements of religious orientation that the great majority of Americans share' (Bellah 1970, p. 171). This sphere amounts to civil religion – a higher order of transcendental reference which allegedly provides legitimation for the nation's highest political and judicial authority. This is the proposed solution of the conundrum that the Federal Constitution separates church and state *but* requires a religious warrant for the separation.

The differentiation of religion from other social institutions, the principled separation of religion from law and politics and the tolerance of religious diversity were not, then, treated by Parsons as evidence of secularization. In fact, even the institutionalization of distinctly secularist outlooks is counter-intuitively said to indicate that both religion and secularism contribute in similar ways towards solving problems of meaning and are, therefore, part of the religious function. According to Parsons, the social system tends to ensure that neither of them can predominate permanently over the other; and they both operate within the framework of values derived from ascetic Protestantism which have guided US culture since its formative period.

The religious 'revival' of the mid-twentieth century in the USA confirmed Parsons in the belief that the case for secularization had been overstated, but he was well aware of the objections to his line of reasoning. Thus, he conceded that the growing popularity of organized religion in the 1950s might have been associated more with a search for sociability and psychological security than with theological beliefs, but he insisted that the central concern was allegedly still with values at a high level of abstraction. And the shift towards such religious concerns was regarded as a structural response to the preceding phase of preoccupation with mainly economic matters. Above all, Parsons denied that the cyclical phases of instrumental and transcendental concerns were signs of change in value-commitments. The overarching, religiously inspired, commitment remained to 'instrumental activism' and to universalist norms governing access to rights and life-chances.

Parsons willingly acknowledged that modern religion *appeared* to have lost much of its former influence, but he attributed the losses to differentiation, not secularization. US society was regarded as a basically Christian society in which the character and expression of religion had admittedly changed in accordance with economic, political and social changes. But the prevailing values were still identified with ascetic Protestantism. Consequently, the growing diversity of religion and the continuing presence of secularism were not considered to be incompatible with the persistence of the religious function. On the contrary, Parsons actually claimed that they were becoming progressively better integrated into a viable cultural system within US society. The structure of that society may have changed, but its basic values had not altered.

### THE PARSONIAN LEGACY IN THE SOCIOLOGY OF RELIGION

It is in the nature of classics in sociological theory to make broad generalizations about such things as societal evolution, types of society and the forces of social change. The wide scope of their generalizations and their ambitious claims to explanatory power, no less than their silences and omissions, ensure that the classics will also be essentially contestable (Alexander, 1987). It is therefore questionable whether theoretical arguments relating to the classical texts can ever be resolved by appeal to, or by discovery of, empirical facts. Indeed, the distinction between theoretical statements and empirical facts is itself contestable. In the circumstances, a more constructive approach to classic texts is to regard the task of interpreting them as open-ended, albeit influenced by prevailing interests and values. The meaning of classics can only be regarded as provisional and relative to the interpreter's own perspective. Ideally, then, discussion should lay bare the theoretical assumptions underlying both the classical texts and the interpreter's position. A limited kind of clarification takes place in the course of such discussion.

In the case of Talcott Parsons's work, we are dealing with a composite *modern* classic which, in turn, selectively synthesized components of earlier classics. This amounts to a double layer of interpretation and is part of the reason for the continuing success of the Parsonian perspective. Parsons was thereby able to persuade many of his contemporaries that, by working within the terms of his theoretical framework, they would also be conducting research which was relevant to the earlier classics. This no doubt contributed strongly to the feeling that the framework was somehow necessary, natural and timeless. It was also felt that empirical investigations were the most appropriate means of demonstrating the framework's relevance to contemporary phenomena.

Parsons's treatment of US religion cannot be separated from his broader concern with the character of modern industrial society. Indeed, the institution of religion plays a major role in his depiction of the general orientation of this type of society and of the motivation that he attributed to its members. And, although only a relatively small part of his writings was specifically about religion, many of Parsons's students and other sociologists whose training had been heavily influenced by his ideas about industrial society were inspired to study religious phenomena from the perspective of normative functionalism. As a result, the sociology of religion in the USA was dominated in the 1950s and 1960s by a concern with: religion as an aspect of socialization; the problem of legitimation; the process of privatization; the relationship between religion and modernization; the nature of religious commitment; and the professionalization of religious leadership roles. The selection of each of these broad areas of concern was strongly conditioned by the distinctively Parsonian model of the modern social system.

It must be emphasized, however, that Parsons's own contributions to this model did not escape criticism and were partly in competition with the ideas of scholars who stood more in the mainstream tradition of anthropological structural functionalism such as R. K. Merton, W. Moore and K. Davis.

The only reasons for attaching so much separate importance to Parsons's action theory here are that it constituted the single most important influence on a generation of sociologists (Gouldner, 1971, p. 168) and that it gave the widest scope for sociological theorizing about the place of religion in modern social systems. It therefore served as the main point of reference for many sociologists of religion in the 1960s without, however, being the only influence on them.

By comparison, many other models of industrial society at that time shared the same structural, functionalist and evolutionary assumptions but tended to be silent when it came to questions of cultural values and religion. William Faunce, for example, characterized industrialism in terms of 'rapid social change, extensive structural differentiation, a low level of social integration, and increased rationalization' brought about mainly by 'change in production technology' (Faunce, 1968, p. 38). The 'hallmarks of industrial society' were said to include:

> a complex division of labor, an occupationally based stratification system, and rationalized procedures for achieving social integration . . . [T]hese attributes are basic structural characteristics of industrial societies and . . . they are directly or indirectly consequences of economic growth, mechanization, and increasing scale of organization.
>
> (Faunce and Form, 1969, p. 3)

And, from a different ideological position, Kerr and associates (1960) based their characterization of the logic of industrialism on increments in the following: a skilled and disciplined workforce; high degrees of occupational and social mobility; high levels of general education; a highly differentiated structure of occupational roles; urbanization; corporatist relations between managers, workers and government; pluralism and consensus in core values; and integration into international networks of industry.

It must also be emphasized that not all sociologists of religion were persuaded of the usefulness of either normative or structural functionalism. Eister (1957), for example, believed that the theoretical specification of the functions of religion was much more problematic, for logical reasons, than was generally acknowledged. And Birnbaum (1955) accused some normative functionalists of reconstructing reality to suit their own biases. But the dominant line of sociological reasoning about religion in the 1950s and 1960s was strongly influenced by the kind of normative and structural functionalist assumptions which pervaded the treatment of religion in popular textbooks by Davis (1949), Nottingham (1954 and 1971) Goode (1951), and O'Dea (1966).

On at least one point, however, Parsons was in agreement with most of his fellow-students of the distinctiveness of industrial society; he believed that economic considerations must at some time have had primacy over others in every to-be-industrial society. And his understanding of economics in industrial society was heavily dependent on Alfred Marshall's orthodox concepts and theories. But he characteristically refused to take economic considerations out of the wider contexts provided by his social action theory. Thus, it was important for Parsons to investigate the conditions in which primacy among the components of a social system could be determined by non-economic factors. Research and education, for example, were clearly regarded as important, but 'value commitments', especially high motivation for achievement, were considered as first prerequisites for industrialization. Thus, 'the institutionalization of a system of values, when internalized in the personalities of individuals, can motivate sufficient "drive" for economic production to carry through the immense labor of industrialization' (Parsons, 1960b, p. 139). Conversely, the main obstacle to economic development was held to be resistance to changing a society's core norms and values in such a way that they would elicit and reinforce 'the motivation to *achievement* in occupational roles devoted to productive functions' (Parsons, 1960b, p. 140). The Judaeo-Christian tradition (and particularly ascetic Protestantism) was believed to encourage values which favoured industrialization, whereas Asian religious traditions were considered inimical or indifferent. Similarly, the Western European systems of Roman Law and Common Law, along with governmental agencies which permitted mobility of people and resources, were also considered more compatible with core values motivating people towards high levels of productivity than were, for example, tzarist regimes and patriarchates.

The universalistic thrust of Parsons's theoretical system was faithfully mirrored in the work of some leading sociologists of religion. For example, Thomas O'Dea's (1963) conceptualization of the paradoxes of institutionalization in religion acknowledges the general influence of Parsons as well as his specific formulation of the 'dilemmas of institutionalization' in *The Social System*. It complements Parsons's depiction of the Hobbesian problem of order with the 'Bergsonian' problem of reconciling spontaneity with stability, or creativity with continuity in the stable evolution of social systems. In particular, O'Dea illustrated his argument about this allegedly 'fundamental functional dilemma for social systems' with the example of innovation in religion. But it was only in respect of the fifth dilemma that O'Dea recognized that religion, as a social phenomenon, was necessarily related to other aspects of society and that there might therefore be the possibility of excessive collaboration between the institutionalized authority system of the religious body and that of the general society (1963, pp. 84–5). The implicit assumption was that the stability of society, as a system guided by norms and values, required a harmonious balance to be struck between the forces of 'pure' religion and purely worldly concerns – a point amplified in O'Dea's textbook (1966).

A similar concern with the functional prerequisites of any social system but with the additional and paradoxical tendency for the pursuit of purely religious goals to result in the growth of a compromised religious organization, the perpetuation of which becomes its major goal, ran through Paul M. Harrison's (1959 and 1960) influential studies of US Protestant denominational structures. The result was a fruitful combination of ironic insights, mainly drawn from Parsons and Weber, into the dynamics of bureaucracy in a religious organization in which authority was simultaneously legitimated on 'rational-pragmatic', 'quasi-charismatic' and 'mimetic-traditional' grounds. The fact that Harrison focused his study on authority and power reflects a more direct link with Weber's interests than with Parsons's theoretical framework.

Parsons had a more direct influence, however, on the form of various studies of modernization and, in particular, of the normative and motivational changes which were believed to precede or accompany it. The best-known studies include R.N. Bellah's (1957) analysis of the anti-modern ideology of the Tokugawa period in Japan and S. N. Eisenstadt's (1968) investigations into the religious motivation towards economic development and modernization.

Bellah (1970) subsequently acknowledged the formative and continuing influence of Parsons's ideas: 'though I have moved away from heavy use of explicitly Parsonian vocabulary and have shifted some of the emphases that can be discerned [in a 1950 paper] . . . I consider my subsequent work more a development than a repudiation of Parsonian theory'. And in his critical reflections on his own study of Japanese religion he admitted that he had not paid sufficient attention to what Geertz called ' "the transformation of the basic structure of society" and its "underlying value-system" ' (Bellah, 1970, p. 57). Furthermore, Bellah's endorsement of certain other scholars' work indicates his approval of the basically Parsonian approach to modernization as the search for evidence of the rationalization of traditional values, in short, a new mentality. For, as is evident in his influential paper on religious evolution, Bellah (1964) takes very seriously the possibility that value systems, the core of which are religious symbols, evolve largely in accordance with an inner logic or dynamic and partly within constraints laid down by circumstances. Thus, 'there was no fundamental tendency toward modernization in Tokugawa Japan' because

> elements of transcendence arose continuously but did not succeed in getting institutionalized, or in gradually penetrating the whole of society. Above all they did not effectively challenge the prevailing particularistic ethic . . . Japan did not have the cultural resources to begin the process of modernization herself.
>
> (Bellah, 1970, pp. 124–5)

By contrast, Bellah argued that the Protestant Reformation in early modern Europe intensified 'pressures to social change in the direction of greater realization of religious values' which were 'actually institutionalized as part of the structure of society itself. The self-revising social order expressed in a voluntaristic and democratic society can be seen as just such an outcome' (Bellah, 1970, p. 39). Religious pressures are therefore credited with developing the modern idea that social systems are, within limits, self-revising; that culture is endlessly revisable; and that personality is continually self-transformable. This is the conclusion of Bellah's investigation of the evolution of religion. The five ideal-typical stages of primitive, archaic, historic, early modern and modern religions are based on illustrative and selective evidence of increasing differentiation and complexity. But no attempt is made to identify any factors which could *explain* the process. A more satisfactory approach was adopted by Parsons in his later work on societies and cultures as cybernetic systems, as we shall see below. The Parsonian inheritance is nowadays clearer, as we shall see in Chapter 4, in the work of Niklas Luhmann than in that of Robert Bellah.

In short, value systems are at the very centre of Bellah's sociology, as they were for Parsons as well. He regarded them as 'more stable and persistent than economic or class forces' (1970, p. 115). Modernization therefore comes to mean construction of social systems 'with a built-in tendency to change in the direction of greater value realization' (Bellah, 1970, p. 39). If this process amounts to a kind of increasing self-awareness and self-direction at the societal level, one wonders whether it would include, for example, the Iranian revolution of 1979, the secularization of Turkey in the 1920s and the Cultural Revolution in China.

Bellah's work on US civil religion (1967) and on the 'broken covenant' (1975) displays a high degree of continuity with normative functionalist analyses of value systems and modernization in industrial society. As we saw above, Bellah considered US civil religion to be an essential, transcendental but critical warrant for the exercise of democratic authority in the USA. The themes of covenant, prophecy, mission and millennium figure prominently in his version of the concept, of which there are, it must be acknowledged, a number of competitors and challengers (see Gehrig, 1981). The principal effect of the US civil religion, according to Bellah, has been to generate powerful symbols of national solidarity and to motivate Americans to attain national goals. The beliefs and rituals that he associates with these symbols and motivations are all regarded as sacred because they allegedly articulate a collective and personal relationship to the ultimate conditions of human existence. For various reasons, however, Bellah (1975) believes that the covenant has not been honoured by the US people. By contrast, others have argued that civil religion is increasingly embodied in public institutions such as law and education. According to Hammond (1980, p. 161), for example, 'Public schools are the new "Sunday Schools" [of civil religion] . . . whereas courts are the new pulpits.' This conception of civil religion's expansion is consequently in tension with Bellah's view that American culture and society are tending towards individualism and privatism (Bellah *et al.*, 1985) and with his stipulation that American civil religion legitimates only those institutions which actually respect the country's fundamental values. In other words, civil religion can judge the state and civil society unfavourably: it is not an unquestionably positive stamp of ideological approval.

We shall return to this tension in Chapter 4, but for the moment it is sufficient to recognize that one of the most direct legacies of Talcott Parsons to the sociology of religion has been a concern with civil religion as a device for coping with the potentially adverse effects of differentiation, pluralism and privatization on the integration of the US social system no less than on the social integration of Americans into rewarding institutions. The functions of civil religion in modern industrial societies seem therefore to be treated as analogous to the functions that Durkheim attributed to the division of labour in society. That is, the fragmentation of communities and the dissolution of traditional social bonds are believed to be counterbalanced by the emergence of moral values and religious symbols of ever wider and more general applicability. Although Bellah resists the idea that US civil religion resembles Durkheim's religion of humanity in its contents, the line of descent from Durkheim to Parsons and to Bellah is clear. The latter's problematic of industrial society has undoubtedly had a decisive influence over the sociological understanding of religion.

Another Parsonian legacy to the sociology of religion is a strong concern with the processes whereby core values, originating and evolving in the cultural system, are institutionalized in social roles and organizations, and internalized in the personality. The implementation of core values at all levels of the action system in a consistent manner was clearly central to Parsons's special understanding of societal functioning. Religion was therefore seen as one of the mechanisms for 'specifying' the most abstract and general values at successively lower levels of what Parsons eventually called the cybernetic hierarchy of the social system. But what if any particular religious organization inculcates values which appear to be inconsistent with the dominant patterns? This was the question which alerted Parsons and some other sociologists of religion to the new-found significance of minority religious sects. Benton Johnson, (1961), for example, reworked much of the earlier theorizing about the sect-type as an apparently other-worldly response to various kinds of deprivation in terms of its actual (if latent) functions as a mechanism of socialization in the 'dominant, institutionalized values of the larger society' (Johnson, 1961, p. 309).

Johnson's research among white members of Pentecostal Holiness churches in North Carolina around 1950 showed that upward social mobility might be a long-term consequence of their inner-worldly ascetic orientation to the world which emphasizes 'individual achievement of concrete goals by the consistent application of appropriate means' (Johnson, 1961, p. 310) and the closely related values of democracy, individualism, mobility and moral respectability. The argument was that, since lower-class white people in the southern states were not typically exposed to these goals and values, the importance that Holiness groups attach to emotional conversion is 'highly suggestive of the fact that these groups endeavoured to reorient the individual's motivations and values in fundamental ways' (Johnson, 1961, p. 311). Moreover, the predominantly ascetic ethos of the Holiness groups was said to mirror the work discipline required for material success in secular occupations. The emotional fervour of the groups' style of worship was, therefore, believed to facilitate the conversion from one outlook to another. The conclusion was that the Holiness emphasis on self-application, consistency and achievement converges with dominant US values.

CONCLUSION

The agenda of US sociology of religion in the 1950s and 1960s was very largely dictated by the normative functionalists' models of the process of modernization and the structure of modern industrial societies. Special emphasis was consequently placed on religion's capacity to mediate the integrative functions of core values, the motivations presumed necessary for 'achievement', the symbols for conveying the USA's prophetic mission of individual liberation and collective prosperity and the ideological means of overcoming such potential sources of social divisiveness as social class, regional culture and racial or ethnic differences. This selective emphasis only makes sense against the background of the normative functionalists' 'landscape' of industrial society.

The landscape began to lose its plausibility in the 1960s, however, when anomalous observations about industrial society and religion began to be registered for the first time. As we shall see in Chapters 4 and 5, doubts were raised about the very form of integration which prevailed in modern social systems. The priority that Parsons and his associates had accorded to values and norms appeared to be unjustified in the light of mounting evidence about the fragmentation of advanced industrial society and about the growing importance of theoretical knowledge in service-based economies. The effects on religion of these transformations were the subject of abstruse, but significant, theorizing by Niklas Luhmann. At the same time, Peter Berger began to express misgivings about the probability that even 'normal' socialization could successfully inculcate personal identity, meaning and order in highly rationalized surroundings. And Thomas Luckmann worked out a theory of socialization which substituted privatized themes of the sacred for the kind of collective values and norms on which the Parsonian theory of modernization had been based. Furthermore, attempts were made, and continue to be made, to save the Parsonian framework's integrity by means of such devices as imperfect socialization, role-strain, latent functions, cultural lag, generational conflicts, collective behaviour and anomie. But the pressure of evidence associated with competing models of industrial, advanced industrial and late-capitalist society has tended to generate more and more grounds for questioning the value of normative functionalism's interpretation of religion.

## NOTE

1   Hadden, 1987, has also noted the interval between the classics and the 'moderns" interest in religion, but I cannot accept his contention that the study of religion was ignored for doctrinaire reasons and that 'Belief in secularization has been sustained by a deep and abiding antagonism to religious belief and various expressions of organized religion' (1987, p. 588). The historical record does not support Hadden's contention.

# 4

# Systems, symbols, societalization, secularization, subjectivity

The normative functionalist model of industrial society which had given rise to various scenarios of the changing significance of religion in the Western world was subjected to conceptual criticism and empirical tests by increasingly large numbers of sociologists in the late 1960s and 1970s. The results were far from unambiguous, but the evidence called for major modifications of the model in certain respects. Many of the taken-for-granted assumptions about secularization and value generalization, for example, were refashioned to accommodate an unexpectedly complex and rapidly changing pattern of religious practice and reported belief (Wuthnow, 1988).

Since they display considerable continuity with Chapter 3, basically functionalist modifications of the Parsonian model of industrial society will be examined at this point. They cast secularization and privatization in a very distinctive light – especially at the hands of Niklas Luhmann. Chapter 5 will examine studies of religion which are in the line of descent from interpretive and phenomenological theories of modernity. And it will conclude with a review of more recent attempts to make sociological sense of religion in terms of structural differentiation and reintegration.

FROM NORMATIVE FUNCTIONALISM TO FUNCTIONAL
SYSTEMS THEORY

Although the essays on religion that Parsons completed in
the latter part of his life (1966 and 1974) have been largely
ignored by commentators, they are nevertheless of a piece
with his earlier work. They are particularly interesting for
indicating that Parsons was able to integrate observations
about the kaleidoscopic changes that were taking place in
Western religion in the 1960s and 1970s into his normative
functionalist framework. In fact, the character of these changes
seemed to chime with the general tendencies of his theorizing
about modernity. In accordance with the cybernetic leanings of
his later work Parsons assigned priority to cultural values and
norms in explaining the processes whereby modern societies
have evolved from earlier types. Moreover, change in these
normative components was construed as evidence of the modern social system's capacity for adaptation to its environment.
In other words, its competitive position was believed to have
improved in the competition for the resources sought by other
neighbouring systems. The adaptive advantage or 'upgrading'
was said to follow from, first, a process of differentiation.
But its success was supposedly conditional, secondly, on the
continuing integration of the differentiated components into
the same overall system. This kind of co-ordination was,
thirdly, considered to be dependent on a process whereby
more generalized norms and values could be shown to be
applicable to each increasingly specialized sub-system or unit.
Again, the long reach of Durkheim's distinctive understanding
of the moral function of the division of labour is evident.

When Parsons applied this perspective to the evolution of
societies, he stressed that

> The dividing criteria, or watersheds, between the major
> stages in our classification [of primitive, intermediate and
> modern societies] center about critical developments in
> the code elements of the normative structures. For the
> transition from primitive to intermediate society, the focal
> development is in language which is primarily a part of the

cultural system. In the transition from intermediate to modern society, it is in the institutionalized codes of normative order internal to the societal structure and centers in the legal system.

(Parsons, 1966, p. 26)

The principal distinctiveness of modern societies, in Parsons's view, lay in the high degree of cybernetic control that could be exercised by means of (1) progressively more specialized normative agencies and (2) increasingly more generalized cultural values which served to lend direction to systematic evolution – differentiation *and* integration, in other words.

These considerations led Parsons to pay increasing attention to the process of value generalization whereby an underlying moral consensus, albeit at ever higher levels of generality, is believed to continue to govern social life at a time when religious pluralism and the declining importance of formal religious organizations have apparently secularized modern industrial society. But the new vehicles of this consensus are said to be the 'intellectual disciplines' such as science and the arts, which have partly replaced 'traditional religion' and kinship as main agencies of socialization. The 'educational revolution' was therefore hailed by Parsons in the early 1970s as the latest stage in the evolutionary process of institutional differentiation and normative integration. The criteria of full membership in the societal community were believed to be increasingly articulated by educational institutions.

This did not mean that religion had been eliminated from public life. Instead, as we saw in Chapter 3, Parsons argued that religion had been given 'a redefined place in the social scene' (Parsons, 1960b, p. 298) as the culmination of a lengthy process of structural differentiation. The implications were, first, that the fundamental values of Americans have roots in religious traditions and have not undergone significant modification in the course of modernization. Secondly, the denominational form of voluntary religious commitment centres on 'the personal intimacy and primacy of the individual's faith and relation to his conception of Divinity' (Parsons, 1960b, p. 312). Thirdly, a regulated competition between secularism and religious forces helps to preserve the freedom of religion and non-religion alike. And fourthly, the aspects of sociability and psychological security which were said to lie beneath the United States' religious revival of the 1950s were regarded as peripheral to the allegedly central phenomenon of increased concern with moral values. Parsons's conclusion was therefore that a reorientation of religion had taken place in the USA but that this did not amount to a weakening of religious values.

Parsons's most general characterization of the reorientated religion of the USA in the early 1970s was of 'a movement that resembles early Christianity in its emphasis on the theme of love' (Parsons, 1974, pp. 210-11). Modern religion is focused on life in the secular world, is relatively non-theistic and is coloured by a sense of alienation, according to Parsons. It is expressed in the search for spontaneous solidarity in experimental living patterns. It also represents a reaction against the rationalization and utilitarian individualism of industrial society but is not a repudiation of the basic US values of 'systematic rational work in "callings" ' (Parsons, 1974, p. 221). Rather, the reorientated religion was part of the shifting balance between the rational-cognitive and affective-expressive components of culture in favour of the latter. Parsons regarded this emergent form of US religion as compatible with Bellah's notion of civil religion and with the continuing stability of industrial society, thereby reasserting his belief that religious change did not necessarily amount to secularization.

In sum, the distinctive meaning of religion in Parsons's interpretation of modernity is inseparable from his understanding of normative systems theory, functional differentiation, value generalization and cybernetic evolution. It amounts to the view that religious values of ever higher generality continue to guide societal development despite the declining power of religious organizations in public life. Religion's impact was said to be mainly at the level of personal identity, motivation and domestic morality. Parsons considered the 'privatization' of religion to be entirely appropriate to life in industrial societies but he denied that it was necessarily secularized in any obvious sense of the term.

The cybernetic and evolutionary perspective on industrial society was reworked by Niklas Luhmann, one of Parsons's students, into an ambitious theory of the changing basis of social order which went well beyond Parsons's normative functionalist framework. In particular, Luhmann raised the theory of social systems to a higher level of abstraction by refusing to model the performance of systems on the rationality of human actors. His style of theorizing is so unusual that we shall have to explicate its basic assumptions before we can assess its implications for an understanding of modern religion.

Whereas Talcott Parsons characterized industrial society by the ascendancy of normative and cognitive considerations over all others, it represents a quite different phenomenon for Luhmann. Luhmann sees the distinctiveness of modern society in the differentiation of its functional systems and sub-systems. As a result,

> Society can no longer be grasped from a single dominant viewpoint. Instead, its dynamic is clarified through the fact that functional systems for politics, the economy, science, law, education, religion, family, etc. have become relatively autonomous and now mutually furnish environments for one another.
>
> (Luhmann, 1982, p. xii)

Luhmann does not simply use the insights of systems theory to explain the distinctiveness of modern Western societies but he actually attributes the latter's distinctive features to their particular type of (self-referential) operations.

According to Luhmann, the main principle of differentiation in pre-modern societies was hierarchical ranking or stratification. But modern society is primarily differentiated on the basis of functional specialization and therefore lacks a unifying principle such as hierarchy. In the absence of hierarchy, functionally differentiated society possesses no symbol of its own unity or identity. Instead, 'Every activity in a system finds its legitimacy in the fact that it is made possible through other activities of the same system. Systems of functions can only legitimate themselves' (Luhmann, 1987, p. 108). Modern society cannot find legitimacy outside its systems, above them, or in the shape of values running through them all. Instead, functionally differentiated systems are self-legitimating in the sense that their meaning is generated exclusively in the course of their own activity. The differentiation between systems of actions makes it impossible for any one of them to represent the total social order.

Despite some evident continuities of thought, the break with Parsonian theory is clearly evident in Luhmann's very conception of a system as a pocket of relatively simple meaning in a relatively more complex environment. Systems remain systems to the extent that the difference in degree of complexity between them and their environment is preserved. The relative simplicity of meaning, action and communication within a system is created and sustained by strategies which allow it to respond to only a selection of all the possible inputs from its environment. Systems selectively filter the complexity of their environment by imposing their own meanings (i.e. reductions of complexity). The function of systems, according to Luhmann, is to reduce complexity by maintaining boundaries between the infinite possibilities of meaning in the world and the selective reductions of meaning in the systems.

Luhmann's understanding of system is considerably more abstract than Parsons's. It treats human beings as the environment of social systems and sub-systems: not as their agents. Thus:

> even the members of an association belong as persons to the environment. They are not really parts of the system. If we give up the old idea that social groups 'consist' of persons and if instead we observe . . . that they are composed of actions as their elementary units, it follows automatically that persons are never entirely incorporated into a social system. Instead, only particular actions of theirs are entangled in particular social systems.
>
> (Luhmann, 1982, p. 42)

This has led one commentator to summarize Luhmann's radical idea as follows: 'Sociology has nothing to do with human beings

as such. It consists of a theory of how they communicate'
(Schöfthaler, 1984, p. 192). In Luhmann's own words, actors
are not the subjects of functional systems theory: 'the action
system is the subject of the agents' (Luhmann, 1982, p. 50).

Actions and meanings are the stuff of communication within
and between systems. Communication is conducted by means
of 'generalized symbolic media' such as truth, love, law,
money, trust and power. They have distinctive symbolic
codes which permit the transfer and exchange of meanings.
'Politics works with power, science with truth, the economy
with money, the family with love' (Luhmann, 1984, p. 45). But,
as religion has historically been internalized and subjectivized,
it cannot attain the same degree of specialization as the other
communication media. Religion functions differently from the
other media by maintaining that, despite structural differentiation, there are still meanings which can be shared by all people.

To appreciate Luhmann's understanding of the place of religion in modern society it is necessary to explicate his general
notion of evolution. It refers to differentiation not just as a
process but also as a shift in the principle on which differentiation takes place, i.e. from segmentation, through stratification
to specialization on the grounds of functional competence. In
the case of religion, Luhmann's argument is that when the
principle of differentiation was segmental, religion functioned
at the societal level by making everything sacred. It was
therefore practised through ritual, cult and eventually myth.
In time, however, and especially when the principle of differentiation became stratification (or integration on the basis of
position in a hierarchy), religion was practised more through
obedience to intellectualized truths (dogmas) and their social
carriers. But when the principle of differentiation became
functional specialization in the modern era, the practice of
religion shifted again in the direction of a personal choice of
increasingly numerous and complex beliefs and devotions.

At each stage of this religious evolution there is a recipro-
cal determination between religion and society of the degree
of complexity displayed by both of them. In other words,
evolution produces a series of progressively more finely differentiated sets of meanings (or reductions of complexity) *and*

progressively more complex environments composed of other sets of meanings. Thus, early religion is considered to be a relatively simple system which creates, and corresponds to, an equally simple view of the world's meaning. By contrast, modern religion is a highly complex sub-system of the social system which treats the world as an equally complex environment of other systems. Consequently, religion is no longer an immediate or obvious 'given' of social life; rather, it may now be either chosen or not chosen. It has therefore become optional, and the choice is presumably made in conjunction with the pattern of choices made in other systems.

As the differentiation of the social system advances, according to Luhmann, there is less need for a religion which is centred on symbolic representations of the totality: 'The *whole* becomes significant only *occasionally*; it is a part in itself' (Luhmann, 1984, p. 8, original emphasis). But the systemic function of religion necessarily persists. That is, interpretation of the meaning of the increasingly complex, differentiated world is regarded as a constant feature of human society. The reason that Luhmann gives for this is that all meaning is paradoxical in the following sense: communication produces redundancy of meanings by showing that things can always be different. A proposition is only meaningful against a background assumption that the facts could have been otherwise. This is what Luhmann means by the world's *contingency*. But the human situation is also paradoxical because it assumes that the world is *necessarily* contingent. There is no escape, then, from the circularity and tautologous nature of communications, the meaning of which is dependent on other meanings. Another way of putting this is to say that meaning can only derive its sense from other meanings, although communication proceeds as if there were in fact fixed points of reference from which certainty of meaning is derived. All social systems face the problem of giving an ultimate meaning to meaning. Attempts are made to solve the paradox in the form of religion. The function of religion for Luhmann is to forestall the danger of an infinite regress of meanings. Religious forms do this by referring to 'contingency formulae' such as God or karma. These formulae explain simultaneously why things have to happen the way they do *and* that they could always be different.

Luhmann considers socio-cultural forms like rituals, myths and dogmas which encapsulate attempts to deparadoxify meaning in this way as, by definition, religious. He also regards the history of religion as the history of differentiations of these religious forms. This is important because it implies that the formation of any society is dependent on the creation of meanings which introduce order into potentially infinite disorder. This represents the general religious function of supplying 'assumptions about the world and bases of interpretation which enabled its definability to be subordinated to moral conduct' (Luhmann, 1974, p. 48). But, as the process of differentiation within religion and within the social system generates finer and finer distinctions between separate sub-systems, the religious function itself becomes institutionalized in a relatively separate sub-system of meaning and action. Just as it becomes possible to choose between different religious meanings, so it also becomes possible to be a member or non-member of religious organizations.

The increasing complexities and indeterminacies of religious meanings, according to Luhmann, were a necessary pre-condition for the transition to 'bourgeois society' in economics and politics. It was only after theology had progressively refined and systematized such ideas as God, karma, revelation and personal salvation on the basis of personal choice that it became possible to conceive of the contingency of the world as amenable to *deliberate* transformation. This is why Luhmann takes the evolution of religious dogmatics to be crucial for the development of the modern world. In this way, Luhmann replaces the moral and motivational pre-conditions that Parsons and other normative functionalists stipulated for the emergence of industrial society by the more formal and intellectual factor of religious dogma.

The shift from moral and motivational to dogmatic factors is accompanied by a different understanding of social pathology. Whereas the normative functionalists have tended to see incomplete or unsatisfactory socialization as the basis for social disorder, Luhmann suggests that the problem lies in the inability of the dogmatic system to react to the change of generations. Yet, he seems to remain open to the possibility that dogmatic theology may still contain untapped capacity, even in modern society, to generate fresh meanings for new generations.

By comparison with much functionalist theorizing about religion, Luhmann's work is less pessimistic about the future of industrial society. His relative equanimity follows from the belief that the evolutionary process of differentiation proceeds on the basis of its own dynamic or inner logic. But it is not a necessary or inevitable development. Moreover, its causes are accidental and unpredictable. It cannot therefore be seen as a regrettable regression from some earlier 'golden age' of communal and consensual solidarity. Luhmann regards the increasing complexity of the world as normal and not a cause for metaphysical pathos. He tends, in fact, to take the formal stability of the social system more or less for granted whilst also recognizing that everyday life and long-term structural transformations can be experienced as conflictual and bewildering. His sanguine attitude probably follows from his assumption that social systems, as systems, tend towards stability precisely *because* of (rather than in spite of) their flexibility and susceptibility to differentiation.

Luhmann's systems theory is relatively free from suggestions that a new term is needed to characterize the nature of present-day social life. The term 'industrial society' is still adequate for his purposes because it serves in his theory as nothing more than a general indication that social systems and, by definition, their environments are significantly more differentiated and complex than they were in the equally vaguely identified pre-industrial society. Indeed, Luhmann has been criticized for failing to explain adequately why the principle of differentiation has supposedly changed from segmentation to stratification and finally to functional specificity. This change is crucial to his theory, but he fails to explain it fully. One possible implication of Luhmann's relative neglect of this part of his theory is that the process of differentiation is a constant and constitutive feature of social systems and does not therefore merit special analysis in itself. In other words, there is nothing unique or even special about present-day social systems; Luhmann regards their differentiation and complexification as merely an effect of dynamics which have operated in all known societies.

It follows from Luhmann's understanding of religion's function in defining and continually redefining a world which is, itself, also undergoing continual change that the function is indispensable. Although many of the tasks previously accomplished by religion have been redefined as the competence of other sub-systems, this does not mean that the religious function has been weakened. It merely means that sub-system boundaries have been redrawn. But, according to Luhmann, the need for conscious reflection on the grounds of all meaning persists. In the absence of any satisfactory way of symbolizing the whole system within any of its parts, legitimacy is generated by the sub-systems *not* in terms of their separate contributions towards the functioning of the whole system but, rather, in terms of their capacity to continue performing their own activities. Thus, the legitimacy of the medical sub-system can only be framed in terms of its capacity to supply further medical services. What sub-systems do is therefore taken as a sufficient justification in itself. Luhmann therefore defines modern social systems as self-referential (and paradoxical) because 'We live in a society without a summit and without a centre. The unity of society no longer comes out in this society' (Luhmann, 1987, p. 105). The paradox is resolved, however, in the idea that

> every activity in a system finds its legitimacy in the fact that it is made possible through other activities of the same system. Systems of functions can only legitimate themselves . . . We are, to use the current terminology, in a hopeless 'legitimation crisis'. What is lacking is not, however, a real legitimation but rather a better insight into the particularity of our societal system.
>
> (Luhmann, 1987, p. 108)

According to Luhmann, the differentiation of modern societal systems has had the effect of turning religious meanings progressively in on themselves. They are no longer identical with meanings attributed to the world, the human world, or whole societies and collectivities. Instead, religious dogmatics have progressively selected the individual person as the operative unit in terms of which conscious reflection on meaning can take place. The language for this self-reflection is that of *faith*. It combines symbols in a distinctive pattern which is not shared by such other special media of communication as love, power, truth and art. Religion, as a sub-system, performs activities for the societal system and for other sub-systems through the medium of the language of faith. That is, activities of other sub-systems will either be selected and supported for being compatible with religious meanings, or they will be rejected because they are incompatible. This is how Luhmann understands interchanges between sub-systems.

The long-term effect of differentiation on the religious sub-system, according to Luhmann, is to engender higher and higher levels of abstraction in the attempt to preserve the identity of religious meanings without, at the same time, jeopardizing the possibility of communicating with, and thereby influencing, the meanings and activities of other sub-systems. Abstraction is seen as a response to increasing complexity in the whole environment of sub-systems. Dogmatics, defined as 'those intellectual concepts which sort, process, control, and systematize religious experiences and situational interpretations' (Luhmann, 1984, p. 49), are therefore credited by Luhmann with much greater significance for the religious sub-system and for the societal system than they assume in other sociological analyses of religion. Many of his writings on religion are in fact devoted to the patterns of correspondence between the development of Christian dogmatics since Late Antiquity and the structural transformation of Western social structures. The binary logic of differentiation and the associated concepts of contingency, abstraction, communication and self-reference are applied equally to both topics.

Just as a systems-theoretical understanding of differentiation avoids both the metaphysical pathos associated with some structural and normative-functionalist interpretations of the fate of religion in industrial societies *and* the moral ethnocentrism of normative functionalism's high expectations of religion's ability to integrate modern societies, so Luhmann's approach is sanguine about the long-term consequences for religion of continuous systematization and abstraction. He does not regard the progressive intellectualization of religious values, ideas, sentiments, rituals, roles and organizations as a regression from a 'golden age' of faith. The concrete ways of fulfilling religion's function have changed, he admits, and there may be many functional equivalents; but there is no question of religion losing its function or of being squeezed into irrelevance by other sub-systems. On the contrary, the systematization of dogmatics is regarded as a guarantee of religion's distinctiveness and separation from an environment in which the failure to differentiate internally and externally would signify absorption into other sub-systems or inability to influence them. Contrary to many exponents of Max Weber's ideas about the disenchantment of the world, for example, Luhmann is able to accept with relative equanimity the facts about the intellectualization of religion; but he also casts their meaning in an entirely fresh light by arguing that symbols of enchantment belong to primarily segmented societies and are incompatible with the prevailing principle of functional differentiation in modern societies. Intellectualization does not therefore signify 'accommodation' to the world; it means that religion has selected meanings which are also shared by many other sub-systems. It is only by means of this kind of symbolic compatibility that religion can possibly influence its environment. The corollary is that religion would lose this influence if its meanings were based on entirely idiosyncratic symbols.

Part of the flexibility that Luhmann claims for his approach is the result of his refusal to follow the example of Talcott Parsons, who identified religion as that part of the social system which was said to have a special relationship with the component of the systemic environment called 'ultimate reality' (Luhmann, 1984, p. 103). Parsons's approach makes religion only a partial system which is specially linked to a partial environment. But Luhmann prefers to think of religion as performing a necessary function on the level of the societal system. That is, it handles a problem common to all systems –

the determinability of the world. The way in which the problem is tackled reflects changes in both religion and its environment; in fact, of course, they mutually shape and constrain each other in a relationship of double contingency. This is all the more reason, for Luhmann, to avoid theoretical formulations which might hypostatize the notion of environment or which might tie religion down to the sphere of ultimate reality.

### FROM NORMATIVE FUNCTIONALISM TO COGNITIVE ORDERLINESS

The Parsonian synthesis of classical theories of industrial society gave pride of place to the idea that Christian norms and values provide the motive power, the direction and the steering mechanism for modern societies. Moreover, these normative components were believed to be essential for societal stability and survival. Parsons implied that it was the social system's need for order which called for the institutions of morality and religion. This is, therefore, a 'top-down', normative functionalist model of the processes whereby the social system allegedly achieves its ends.

Equally synthetic, but different, ideas about the place and meaning of religion in modern societies were also produced by other theorists in the 1960s. But the best known of the non-Parsonian theorists, Peter Berger and Thomas Luckmann, approached the question of religion from the 'bottom up'. Leaving aside the functionalism of Berger's *The Noise of Solemn Assemblies* (1961a), their approaches have generally lacked the Parsonian accent on systemicity and normative functionalism. Instead, they emphasized the processes of social interaction and symbolization by means of which individuals and groups of people construct meaning. To the extent that Berger and Luckmann implied that human beings *needed* to construct meaning, there is a note of psychological functionalism in their ideas. But their joint and separate writings contain no suggestion that modern societies are systems with imperative needs for order. Rather, social, moral and religious order is explained as an outcome of individual human beings' striving for meaning, legitimation and security. In this perspective, order in society is first and foremost an emergent product of social interaction.

It is an open question whether Berger and Luckmann synthesized classical sociological perspectives into a new *theory* of industrial society. What matters more for present purposes is that their theoretical ideas, which are probably not articulated methodically enough to warrant the label of theory, pursue selected themes from the classics and weave them loosely into a distinctive perspective on modernity. But the term 'industrial society' has no special significance in their work. This is because the weight of their analysis is on cultural matters, that is, questions of meaning, consciousness, language and symbol. In so far as Berger and Luckmann have analysed patterns of social relationships, their primary aim has been to explain *cultural* phenomena by reference to the social structures and processes which sustain them.

The influence of Kant, Hegel and Heidegger, no less than that of these philosophers' intellectual heirs, Max Weber and Alfred Schutz, is apparent in Berger and Luckmann's orientation towards the meaning of modernity as it is generated in social interaction and experienced in the consciousness. This phenomenological turn of German social thought is blended with some of Marx's insights into the dynamics of conflict and competition between social classes. And, particularly in Luckmann's perspective on religion, extensive use is made of Durkheim's understanding of the *sui generis* nature of social reality. The mixture of intellectual sources is completed with G. H. Mead's social psychological appreciation of the social process of self- and identity-formation. The result of this admixture of such diverse theoretical ideas is an unquestionably innovative synthesis, although it is only in Berger's most recent work to date (1986) that the first signs of a theory, in the sense of a logically interrelated set of general propositions, can be found.

Berger and Luckmann have shared so many ideas in common that it makes sense to introduce their sociological analyses of modernity without regard for the differences which can be found between the two scholars' ideas. Nevertheless, I shall treat them separately from this point on because it is in their views on religion that some of the most significant differences between the two scholars are apparent. Indeed, following their jointly written article on secularization and pluralism (1966b), Berger and Luckmann have taken different paths towards a sociological understanding of religion, albeit in the same general direction of a cultural analysis of modernity, its discontents, possibilities and sources of resistance.

### MODERNITY AND THE TWO KINGDOMS

Peter Berger has written so much about religion in such a subtle style that it is not easy to summarize his arguments briefly. An added difficulty is that his ideas continue to evolve, and his personal involvement in religious activities shows no sign of waning. On the other hand, there are no major breaks in the continuity of his thought. Apart from his second thoughts about the value of functionalist definitions of religion (1974a), Berger's thinking about religion has not deviated significantly from the problems and principles which guided his earliest work. The central concern has always been, and continues to be, with the social, cultural and experiential implications of the process of rationalization. Of course, there are many improvisations on this theme; and he has applied it to increasingly diverse topics. But the strength of the underlying thematic links is greater than the diversity of applications.

Beginning in the mid-1950s with his PhD dissertation on the Baha'i religion, and continuing through his early publications on sectarianism, the problems of Christian community in the modern world, Israelite prophecy and the market-like context of ecumenism, Berger's work was focused on the paradox that rationality in the Western world has religious origins but is also corrosive of the kind of communities which have traditionally nurtured religious ideas and feelings. The main implications of rationality for modern Christian denominations were said to be pluralism, that is, the erosion of the monopoly which religious organizations had traditionally enjoyed over legitimate world-views, the progressive segmentation of religious and non-religious outlooks and the weakening of taken-for-granted assumptions in the life-world about self-identity, moral virtue and religious truth. Moreover, competition for plausibility between pluralistic religious groups and between religious and non-religious groups allegedly generates further rationalization of the groups' methods of increasing their share of the 'market'. Ecumenism, 'cartelization' and bureaucratization are similarly regarded as rationalized responses to the market situation of pluralistic religion. They, in turn, are associated with rational strategies for increasing the marginal differentiation of religious 'products', albeit within a market which favours the standardization of consumer preferences. This is all congruent with Berger's depiction of secularization as 'the process by which sectors of society and culture are removed from the domination of religious institutions and symbols' (1967, p. 107) and as the production of increasing numbers of people 'who look upon the world and their own lives without the benefit of religious interpretations' (1967, p. 108). Berger held that the problem of meaninglessness was intimately related to the effects of secularization on the level of social structures and consciousness alike.

Let me be more precise at this point about Berger's way of accounting for the social and cultural distinctiveness of modernity. It is not an idealist or historicist theory about the development of reason in the abstract. Nor does it claim that the process of rationalization is historically inevitable or mechanical. The argument is, rather, that once the idea of consistently seeking an efficient relationship between means and ends was seen to confer advantages, material and intellectual forces have been mobilized in its pursuit. From its origins in Ancient Judaism and despite the desecularizing force of Roman Catholicism, the notion of rationality was boosted by the Protestant Reformation and the Renaissance until, in the early modern world, it acquired an autonomy and a dynamic of its own. The process of rationalization is therefore regarded by Berger as open-ended but variable in pace of development and degree of impact on different parts of society and culture.

Berger's characterization of the modern world actually gives priority to the way in which *technological* rationality induces economic growth and thereby shapes social institutions. In particular, bureaucracy is regarded as one of the most salient institutions of modernity and is analysed on many occasions for its impact on human values and consciousness. This is not a technological determinism, however, since Berger also recognizes that social and cultural resources may be employed to resist or canalize the effects of technology.

Around the mid-1960s Berger's concern with rationalization and modernity increasingly found expression in analyses of personal identity and consciousness. His view was that the growth of bureaucracy, in association with economic growth, had created a widening gulf between the public world of state, politics and work and the private world of family, community and self. Following Arnold Gehlen, he argued that the big institutions of the public realm were invading the private sector and depriving its institutions of meaning. Religion, which had previously supplied an overarching canopy of supernatural meaning for both public and private realms, was unable to prevent this 'de-institutionalization' of the life-world because religion had already become segmented and pluralized. As a result, Berger came to fear that modern consciousness would be more and more dominated by the rational logics of politics, business and employment. But they are not adequate, in his view, for the task of giving people stable identities and satisfying ideas about the meaning of life and the explanation of suffering and death. In short, he claimed that the most powerful institutions of the modern world had lost their moral and religious legitimation: the articulation between public and private had supposedly broken down. But, as I shall show below, Berger's later writings argue that capitalism can, in any case, only be legitimated in terms of its material achievements, and not in ideological terms.

Berger tends to treat the private sphere as a residual category of experiences and social relations which are not dominated by the rationality of formal management and economic production. Separation from the public sphere has allowed personal preferences in lifestyle to proliferate to the point where previously obligatory beliefs and practices have now become purely optional. The *necessity* to make choices ('the heretical imperative'), according to Berger, can therefore be experienced as alienating and confusing no less than as liberating.

Much of Berger's work in the 1970s and 1980s has been concerned precisely with ways of understanding and overcoming the allegedly alienating effects of modernity. Pride of place must be given to his belief that the disabling gulf between the public and the private can only be bridged by the creation of social structures which could charge private individuals with the capacity to control public institutions. These intermediary structures would have to make certain beliefs plausible and to mediate between the levels of individuals and society. The thrust of Berger's political and religious strategy is not radically conservative or other-worldly. It is, rather, framed in the spirit of de Tocqueville's and Durkheim's sketches for a democracy of cross-cutting voluntary associations, religious groups, communities and families. The strategy is expected to provide a relatively firm anchorage for personal identity and meaning at the level of consciousness as well as increased legitimation for institutions at the level of society. He is therefore seeking to recover 'the middle ground' from the threats that authoritarianisms and totalitarianisms of both left and right allegedly pose to individual freedom and societal integrity in modernity.

It is quite conceivable that Berger's analysis of modernity and of its corrosive effects on personal identity and meaning could have been produced with little or no reference to religion. After all, there are some close affinities with conservative, non-religious theories of mass society. There are also strong resemblances to, for example, Zijderveld's (1970) depiction of the 'abstract society'. And Berger's analysis of rationality is partly congruent with Habermas's extensive project for combating the destructive effects of instrumental reason on the human life-world. Moreover, the strategy for empowering people through revitalized mediating structures has many parallels in secular social theory. We must be clear, then, about the distinctiveness of Berger's views about the place of religion in modernity. They are distinctive mainly for the underlying tenets of his philosophical anthropology.

The counterpart to Berger's positive assessment of the human capacities to create meaning and order in the process of social interaction is his implicit assumption that humans are surrounded by threatening forces of disorder and chaos. Culture is said to be 'unstable', for example, and the human organism is characterized by a 'built-in instability' (Berger, 1967, p. 5). A memorable passage has it that

> The world is built up in the consciousness of the individual by conversation with significant others (such as parents, teachers, 'peers'). If such conversation is disrupted (the spouse dies, the friends disappear, or one comes to leave one's original social milieu), the world begins to totter, to lose its subjective plausibility. In other words, the subjective reality of the world hangs on the thin thread of conversation.
>
> (Berger, 1967, p. 17)

The socially established *nomos* is considered to be a shield against the 'terror' which allegedly lurks in the marginal situations of life. The *nomos* represents 'an area of meaning carved out of a vast mass of meaninglessness, a small clearing of lucidity in a formless, dark, always ominous jungle . . . Every nomos is an edifice erected in the face of the potent and alien forces of chaos' (Berger, 1967, pp. 23–4). The capacity of religion to keep the existential nightmares at bay is crucial for Berger because the sacred cosmos is said to be designed to confront chaos as its terrible contrary. This Manichaean phenomenology underlies a distinctive interpretation of one of the problems of modernity:

> secularization frustrates deeply grounded human aspirations – most important among these, the aspiration to exist in a meaningful and ultimately hopeful cosmos . . . There are, of course, secular 'theodicies', and they clearly work for some people. It appears, however, that they are much weaker than the religious 'theodicies' in offering both meaning and consolation to individuals in pain, sorrow and doubt.
>
> (Berger, 1977, p. 79)

As I pointed out above, Berger regards bureaucracy and the unremitting search for economic growth as the main corrosive acids of the modern world. They are blamed for separating the public and the private, work and meaning, existence and identity. In each case, impersonal forces of calculating reason are said to have undermined the communities and 'conversations' which previously sustained worlds of meaning and legitimated institutions – especially in view of the grim statement that 'every human order is a community in the face of death' (Berger, 1977, p. 80). The religious mystifications of the humanly constructed world have allegedly been replaced by matter-of-fact arrangements which cannot conceal their very human origins and purposes. As a result, Berger argues that the positive benefits of religious alienation are no longer attainable, and the terrors of anomie are all the more pressing.

Religious pluralism and the market-like structure of relations among competing religious groups in the modern world therefore represent for Berger a very weak substitute for the ancient vehicles of religious credibility. The separation of church and state completes the process of secularization which, ironically, originated in religion and was subsequently accelerated by economic rationality. Indeed, Berger believes that any attempts that religious organizations might make to 'reconquer' the socioeconomic centre of modern industrial societies would 'threaten to dismantle the rational foundations of modern society' (Berger, 1967, p. 132). By contrast, the focus of 'voluntary' religion on the sphere of the relatively fragile nuclear family makes no such threats to modernity: it merely accentuates the segregation of personal meaning or identity from affairs in the public sphere.

The theme of the private/public split assumed greater and greater importance as Berger's writings in the 1970s turned towards Third World issues. His early writings on this topic emphasized two things. On the one hand, Berger regarded the impact of modern industrial and capitalist practices on Third World countries as basically destructive of the social and cultural roots of value, meaning and identity. *The Homeless Mind* (co-authored with Brigitte Berger and Hansfried Kellner in 1973) analysed the disruptions of consciousness and identity wrought by modernity on traditional cultures and social formations. But, on the other hand, the same book held out the hope that religious organizations in Third World countries might be able to mount an effective resistance against the onslaught of modernity. A similar ambivalence towards modernity underlay the essays collected in *Pyramids of Sacrifice* (1974b). It was complicated by an attempt to remain even-handed towards what Berger dismissed as the capitalist myth of growth and the socialist myth of revolution: neither hunger nor terror was considered an acceptable cost of socioeconomic development in the Third World. Instead, he argued that 'intermediate structures', in which 'those who are the objects of policy' would have the opportunity to shape their own future, should be created and sustained even if they are ultimately found to be 'counter-modernizing' (Berger, 1974b, pp. xii–xiii).

Berger (1986) later acknowledged that this attempt to have the best of both worlds ('hardnosed utopianism') was a failure. The even-handed approach therefore yielded to a one-sided debunking of socialism and an equally partial eulogy of the benefits of development in the capitalist mode. The ethical dilemmas associated with Third World development are not so confidently resolved, but capitalism is described as on balance 'the morally safer bet' (1986, p. 12). The grounds for this assessment are given in fifty propositions about the allegedly superior capacity of the capitalist mode of production to generate the highest standards of living, democratic stability, open systems of social stratification, the pre-conditions for individual autonomy and the best chances for increasing prosperity in any kind of society.

If these grounds appear to be uncharacteristically materialist for Berger, he attributes this unexpected turn in his work to the belief that capitalism is incapable of legitimating itself in mythic terms (unlike socialism). He believes that the best case can only be made for capitalism in factual and practical terms. This is why so much emphasis is placed in *The Capitalist Revolution* on the empirical evidence for and against capitalism's capacity to raise standards of living in developed and developing countries alike.

By contrast, Berger (1983 and 1986) claims that the only arguments which support socialism are 'mythic' in the sense that they are founded on deep-seated assumptions and prejudices for which empirical support is non-existent. Socialism, in Berger's view, is inescapably bureaucratic, inefficient, authoritarian and patrimonial. Moreover, he rejects the idea that socialism can be rescued, politically or economically, by the introduction of market mechanisms or other non-socialist devices. For this reason, he dismisses the current vogue in many parts of the developing world for a synthesis of Marxism and Christianity in the form of liberation theology as dangerous and illusory. In fact, Berger perceives a contradiction between the inherent totalitarianism of socialism and the inherent relativism of religion. Nevertheless, he is sufficiently disturbed by the prospect of a viable compromise between religion and Marxism to warn explicitly against the danger of 'the sort of ultimate legitimation of the totalitarian project that will make the latter perdure for centuries' (1986, p. 192).

Above all, there is anxiety in Berger's recent writings about the possibility that the fervent hopes for imminent improvement in the standards of living in Third World countries might acquire a religious, millennial character. This anxiety is aggravated by what Berger claims to be a religious quest or pilgrimage among Western intellectuals for countercultural primitivism and orientalism in the Third World. He inveighs against Westerners who 'use the Third World as the arena for their own spiritual dramas – be it as missionaries or pilgrims – [because they display] an attitude of contempt for the real people of these countries' (1983, p. 195). 'This-worldly messianism' is therefore condemned as 'murderous'. Religious conceptions of the Third World must, in Berger's opinion, be avoided for fear that new forms of Cargo Cult might be stimulated. Instead, he argues that priority should be given to the question of how greater wealth could be *produced* in developing countries. Questions of distribution, transfer, or equity are expected to resolve themselves – but only if 'the spiritual hunger, moral guilt, or ideological dissonances of the West' (1983, p. 196) are not projected on to the Third World in utopian or millennial fantasies.

The lessons of Berger's excursion into the intricacies of Third World politics and economics seem to sit uneasily with his earlier, bland depiction of the social reality of religion as a sacred canopy. A cynic could be forgiven for inferring that Berger would now exclude messianism, millennialism and Cargo Cults from the very category of religion. But this would be an unjust inference. All that has happened in the two decades that separate his treatise on the sociology of religion from his analysis of the precarious condition of the Third World is that an unstated presupposition has become more explicit. A categorical distinction between 'real' religion and politics was concealed in the early work but is now manifest. In effect, the Lutheran doctrine of the two kingdoms has worked itself out in the form of sociological arguments. These arguments were dimly foreshadowed in Berger's earliest books on the state of US denominations (1961a and 1961b). His complaint was that the mainline denominations had failed to voice 'prophetic' criticisms of the problems facing US society. He therefore urged Christians to tackle the task of social criticism seriously – not from secular standpoints, however, but only from theological starting-points. Again, the intention is clearly to keep the religious and political criteria for action separate and not to lose sight of transcendent values in the struggle for mundane results.

Since the treatise on the sociology of religion (Berger, 1967) was narrowly focused on the positive and integrative functions of religion for both individuals and societies, questions of conflict were put aside (Beckford, 1983). Now that events in many parts of the world have threatened to show up the limits of such a perspective on religion, however, Berger has had to turn to an explicit argument which preserves religion's integrity more clearly. This is why he is at pains not only to distinguish between the two kingdoms of religion and politics but also to emphasize the dangers inherent in confusing them. Thus: 'Insofar as *homo religiosus* has been informed by the Judeo-Christian tradition, he does indeed harbor an eschatological hope, but it looks to God and not to the political acts of men for its fulfillment' (1986, p. 223). This quotation reinforces the suspicion that Berger's sociological understanding of religion is heavily coloured by Judaeo-Christian influences, for the categorical separation of religion and politics is inapplicable to most expressions of Islam and to many versions of Hinduism, Buddhism and Shinto. In spite of his disdain for Western intellectuals who have projected their socialistic Utopias on to the Third World, Berger therefore appears to want to impose a narrowly Western, Christian and Lutheran image of religion on the faith communities of those parts of the world where the distinction between religion and politics is meaningless.

In fact, there is a striking irony in Berger's insistence on this distinction. It is simultaneously an instance of the separation between public and private spheres of life (which Berger regrets) and an argument for keeping the spheres separate. The worst scenario for him would probably be for politics to masquerade as religion, or vice versa. The logic of Berger's position therefore compels him to campaign for societal structures in which the categories remain separate but cross-cutting. The intended result is a version of liberal pluralism which derives its stability and dynamism from the checks and balances that the private realm of religion (along with family and community) can impose on the public realm of politics (along with state institutions and formal organizations of business and industry) and vice versa.

In sum, Peter Berger's distillation of the classical sociological theories of industrial society is a complex weave of interpretive, phenomenological, interactionist and structural approaches. It depicts the process of rationalization as the key to social change but it also recognizes that the course of this process is affected by social class, ethnic and national interests. Moreover, the process is not treated as abstract or disembodied; it is, in fact, said to be constantly negotiated between competing interest groups. The struggle to impose particular meanings on social life is the stuff of social interaction and the guarantee that some kind of legitimate order will prevail in the face of the immanent threat of chaos.

In so far as Berger's analysis of modernity adds anything new to the classical problematics of industrial society, it draws attention, first, to the effects of rationalization on individuals' sense of identity and meaning. His most valuable contributions to a sociological understanding of religion probably lie in this area. His sensitive appreciation of the social interactional settings of religious belief and experiences have in fact sparked off many fruitful investigations of modern symbol and meaning systems.

Secondly, his analysis has increasingly emphasized the importance of the relationships of mutual influence between the economically developed and developing countries. Although he is critical of the theories of dependency, the development of underdevelopment and the world-systems, Berger nevertheless believes that the prospects for material well-being and political stability in the developed democracies are in part conditioned by the course of modernization in the Third World and vice versa. The religious implications of this are, on the one hand, that voluntarism and the separation of religion and politics should be encouraged in developing countries, and, on the other, that Western intellectuals should refrain from exporting socialistic and millennial Utopias to the Third World.

And, thirdly, Berger has avoided the temptation to consider his own age as a critical turning-point in human history. Categories such as 'traditional', 'industrial' and 'post-industrial' have very little significance in a perspective which locates the origins of the modern malaise in the dawn of known human history. Thus, although Berger is concerned above all with understanding modernity he traces its characteristic features back to ancient sources of rationalization and secularization. Moreover, the underlying philosophical anthropology, pitting social order and personal identity against chaos and homelessness, remains constant. There are, then, no discontinuities or crucial junctures in Berger's account of societal development: only the continuous process of adjustment between changes in social structures and changes in consciousness. What is more, in comparison with his classical predecessors and with many of his contemporary social critics, Berger remains almost stoically ambivalent towards the evolving character of modernity. In fact, he leaves the impression that, as long as the two kingdoms are kept separate, the threat of both totalitarianism and atomism will be held in abeyance first by the capacity of the supernatural to relativize all human order and secondly by the capacity of voluntaristic religious organizations to mediate between the individual and society. Berger's present belief is that the economic culture of capitalism offers the best prospects for success in producing the material benefits of modernity and in minimizing modernity's pathological costs.

In conclusion, it seems ironic that Berger's highly original and influential interpretations of the causes and symptoms of secularization do not form part of a more conventional scenario of secularization. There is very little pathos in his analyses of, for example, religious pluralism, privatization, or cartelization. Instead, there seems to be confidence that, regardless of what happens to particular religious groups, the social production of order, meaning and identity in a transcendental framework will persist – and not only on the margins of mainstream society, as Daniel Bell (1980) and Bryan Wilson (1979 and 1982) have suggested, but also in influential strata. For all the similarities between Berger's social criticism and that of other social theorists, his reading of modernity is distinguished by an unusual sensitivity to the 'Rumour of Angels'. The metaphysical pathos of most theories of secularization is hardly detectable in his more sanguine assessment of the prospects for religion in the modern world – at least, in the developed capitalist sectors.

### DIFFERENTIATION AND PRIVATIZED RELIGION

If Peter Berger's attitudes towards modernity are more san-guine than those of most classical sociologists and of many present-day social critics, the stance of his erstwhile colleague and co-author, Thomas Luckmann, towards modern society is even less anguished. Luckmann does not appear to share Berger's misgivings about the problem of psychological home-lessness or anomie, nor do his writings express fears about the prospects for the collapse of free and orderly democracies into totalitarianism. And his publications give no grounds for inferring that he shares Berger's faith in the capacity of voluntaristic religious organizations to stave off social chaos by mediating between otherwise atomized individuals and the impersonal social structures of modern societies. Luckmann's work actually represents a radical extension of the type of diagnosis found in the classical problematics of industrial society and mass society. It is founded on a different, more humanistic, philosophical anthropology than the one which underlies Berger's vision of human society as a 'community in the face of death'.

Thomas Luckmann is probably best known in the English-speaking sociological community for introducing it to Alfred Schutz's phenomenological sociology of the life-world. His co-authorship with Peter Berger of their widely read *The Social Construction of Reality* (1966a) was another aspect of the same phenomenological project. But relatively few sociologists outside the sociology of religion are familiar with Luckmann's most original work, *The Invisible Religion* (1967), a shorter version of which first appeared in German in 1963. Although the book is a sustained analysis of what Luckmann called 'the problem of religion in modern society', its scope is actually much wider. It amounts to an interpretation of the changing relationships between social structures, consciousness, culture and personal identity in the modern world. This is why he has often been at pains to situate his work in the framework of a sociology of knowledge which would go beyond the history of ideas and penetrate the central sociological question of how human beings are located in their social order. For both Berger and Luckmann, in fact, 'the most important task' of the sociology of religion 'is to analyze the cognitive and normative apparatus by which a socially constituted universe (that is, "knowledge" about it) is legitimated' (Berger and Luckmann, 1963, p. 424).

The striving for a sociology of knowledge approach to religion is entirely characteristic of Luckmann's work and is reflected in his many publications on language, world-views and consciousness. But within this set of topics religion occupies pride of place because of Luckmann's unusual adherence to a rigorously Durkheimian argument that the very relationship between individuals and society is religious. His studies of religion are therefore highly distinctive, not only for their sensitivity to matters of language, consciousness and experience, but also for the strong claims that they make about the centrality of religion to the whole social process.

This is why there is such a strong sense of frustration in Luckmann's early writings with the allegedly trivial character of most sociological analyses of religion. He criticized the taken-for-granted identification of religion exclusively with what happens in formal religious organizations; and he denied that rituals and doctrines exhausted the category of religious phenomena. His argument was that religion is a structural as well as a cultural feature of all societies and that its 'invisible' functions are no less important for not being empirically available for observation and measurement. Thus, the carefully collected evidence of the changing activities of religious organizations, even in cases of undisputed decline, could not shake Luckmann's conviction that religion, as a constituent feature of all societies, was not necessarily experiencing decline.

In other words, the distinction between the strictly sociological category of religion and the everyday phenomena of church-oriented activity allowed Luckmann to deny that the process of modernization was directly responsible for secularization. Churches may have become marginal to the major centres of power and influence, and they may have become 'internally secularized' as a result of bringing their values and beliefs into line with the non-religious norms of the dominant institutions of the economy and the polity. But, Luckmann argued, this evidence of the declining significance of religious organizations merely indicates that the process of institutional differentiation has removed the possibility that traditional religious norms could still legitimate and integrate the social order of industrial societies. The formerly overarching symbols and values are now themselves relegated to a separate institution. According to Luckmann, this does not mean, however, that the broad function of religion is in decline.

On the contrary, Luckmann has consistently tried to make the case that 'meaning systems that relate experiences of everyday life to a "transcendent" layer of reality' (1967, p. 44) continue to locate individuals in their social order and that these 'symbolic universes' therefore fulfil an essentially religious function. He considers this function to be religious because it enables individuals to transcend their 'biological givenness' and thereby to locate their practical actions in a broadly sacred context. But, in a rapidly changing world, he argues, the crystallization of religious world-views into formal religious doctrines and practices introduces a degree of rigidity which may create problems for personal identity. If everyday experiences are inconsistent with fixed religious notions, the resulting tension between 'official' and 'personal' religion is therefore likely to increase, especially from generation to generation.

Again, Luckmann is insistent that the proliferation of personal models of religious reality is not necessarily a sign of the decline of religion; it is only a problem for the plausibility of official, i.e. church-oriented, religion. The broader function of religion in a sociological sense remains no less relevant to modern societies than it has always been in, for example, tribal societies or than it was in the so-called 'ages of faith'. Luckmann is therefore confident, in true Durkheimian fashion, that an institutionally non-specific form of religion is emerging in response to the declining significance of church-oriented religion in modern societies.

It is important to recognize that Luckmann's sketch of the emergent personal religion does not simply propose that the old form will replace the new. He believes that church-oriented religion will persist; but alongside it there will be a radically new form of religion. It will be radically new in the sense of, first, lacking an overarching coherence or structure. Instead, it will consist of an assortment of sacred themes chosen by the individual. Moreover, the selections will express flexible and unstable arrangements of personal priorities which have little or no backing from public institutions. The second novelty is that these themes will not be mediated by special institutions, nor will they necessarily be connected with any other social institutions. They represent consumer preferences and are therefore congruent with the individual's sovereign status and location in modern society. Thirdly, Luckmann argues that the themes originate in the 'private sphere' and are primarily rooted in personal sentiments. But they may also reflect Judaeo-Christian ideas *and* notions which arise from political and economic ideologies.

Luckmann's brief outline of the typical contents of the new, personal religion of modern societies is intriguing but hardly substantial. It suggests that the image of the autonomous individual is dominant and is supported by cognate ideas about the sacred character of self-expression and self-realization. This imagery finds an echo in the celebration of sexuality, familism and the ethos of 'getting along together'. In short, the new form of religion is congruent with modern industrial society without explicitly legitimating it. Its sacred themes and images explain and celebrate the relationships between autonomous individuals and their society. But they do not symbolize, much less integrate, the overall structure of society. To the extent that the new religion of the individual is actually 'religious' in Luckmann's terms it points beyond the biological givenness of the individual and identifies him or her as an autonomous person in a society of specialized and separated institutions, each with its own kind of rationality but without an overarching principle of coherence.

The distinctiveness of Luckmann's analysis of the problem of religion in industrial society lies not so much in his account of the differentiation of institutions and the specialization of religion but more in his argument that these thoroughgoing transformations of church-oriented religion have done little to affect the *function* of religion. This has nothing to do with the psychological 'need' for religion nor with structural functionalist claims about the alleged need for the religious integration of all social institutions. And, although there are some points of agreement with Parsons's understanding of differentiation and adaptive upgrading, Luckmann gives no credence to Parsons's cybernetic theses or to the argument about value generalization. Similarly, there would be no place in his scheme for Niklas Luhmann's abstract ideas about self-referential systems and 'contingency formulae'.

And, finally, Luckmann's distinctive conceptualization of religion sets his diagnosis of the problem of religion in the modern world apart from that of Peter Berger. For, although the two theorists agree on the need to approach religion from the perspective of an interactionist and phenomenological sociology of knowledge, there is a wide gulf between Luckmann's sense of religion as an institution for locating individuals in society and Berger's sense of religion as a framework of supernaturally rooted beliefs and values. Thus, the process of corrosive rationalization which, in Berger's opinion, threatens to destroy the plausibility of religion is only one more factor which, according to Luckmann, transforms the official model of church-oriented religion into an unofficial, personal form of religiosity.

### 'RECULER POUR MIEUX SAUTER'

Talcott Parsons drew together selected themes from classical models of industrial society into a synthesis which argued that religion, in the guise of core values, was central to the functioning of Western societies. Although Parsons placed an unusually heavy emphasis on the importance of religious values to the dynamic of industrial society he was not alone in conceptualizing religion as a prime motivator and regulator of the social system. This enabled him and many sociologists who were influenced by his ideas to believe that industrial societies were converging on a common type of social system but, at the same time, to deny that technology was the sole driving force. According to this general model of industrial society, the declining salience of organized religion goes hand in hand with the growing significance to the total social system of generalized values and privatized identities.

Niklas Luhmann, Peter Berger and Thomas Luckmann all seem to accept some of Parsons's basic assumptions about the processes of institutional differentiation, privatization and rationalization. But none of them agrees with his claim that religious values remain central to industrial society. Rather, their own (very different) perspectives on societal development produce sharply differing interpretations of the place of religion in modernity.

According to Luhmann, the differentiation of social institutions has proceeded so far in industrial society that there is no longer a need for a special institution to represent the unity and the legitimacy of the whole system. He seems to believe that, with the specialization of each major social institution in accordance with its own kind of rationality, it would be theoretically as well as practically impossible for the traditional religious function of system integration to be fulfilled. Organized religion is therefore forced to become more specialized. The logic of Luhmann's systems approach suggests that religious groups will survive in advanced industrial societies by continually monitoring their boundaries with other institutions and by trying to assert their autonomy and distinctiveness. Moreover, individuals can now choose whether to adopt a religious outlook. And the kind of religious consciousness which predominates in advanced industrial societies is said to symbolize ultimate meaning in terms of personal identity: not authoritative dogma. The main problem for modern religion is therefore to allow dogmas to be brought into line with rapidly changing conditions of life as experienced by successive generations of people. What is needed, then, is insight into the dynamics of the social system. The specific language of faith, as the medium of communication that Luhmann attributes uniquely to religion, is said by him to retain the important function of articulating this insight in modern societies. But it is not clear whether he expects formal religious organizations to have a major part in fulfilling this function.

By contrast, Peter Berger's analysis of the dynamics of modernity is less functionalist and more attentive to the structural role that religious organizations are believed to play in countering some of the most destructive tendencies of industrial society. Emphasizing the rationalization of public life and the problematic gulf between the public and private worlds, Berger acknowledges that the canopy of sacred meaning that was formerly cast by religion over all human life is now only a patchwork of largely privatized experiences. Yet, on the other hand, he clings to a philosophical anthropology which not only demands that human beings seek meaning through order but also leaves open the possibility that individuals and groups can choose to mediate between the public and the private. Unlike Luhmann, therefore, Berger regards human beings and their voluntary associations as real actors: not as the mere environment of social systems and sub-systems. As a result, he credits these agents with the capacity to shape the process of rationalization and to overcome some of the worst problems of modern societies, that is, the impersonality and manipulativeness of bureaucracies, the erosion of personal identity, the atomization of privatized experience and the exploitativeness of political and economic ideologies.

Finally, Thomas Luckmann's radically Durkheimian interpretation of religion as the social institution which locates individuals in social structure arises from yet another, different understanding of the dynamics of industrial society. In this case, the emphasis is placed on the secular process of specialization among religious institutions and on the concomitant difficulty of generating stable personal identities based on the notion of individual autonomy. Luckmann makes no proposals, however, for religious organizations to intervene practically in trying to bridge the gap between the public and the private. This is mainly because Luckmann situates the problem of modern society on the level of consciousness rather than on the level of exchanges between, for example, churches and political or economic organizations. In his view, church-oriented religion has been marginalized by structural transformations of industrial society. But the function of ensuring that individuals acquire a sense of their location in society still needs to be fulfilled, in his opinion. Consequently, Luckmann expects new themes of individual autonomy to be generated in everyday social interaction. The problem of religion in modern society has to do, then, with the difficulty of symbolizing individual autonomy at a time when social life appears to be dominated by monolithic public institutions.

Each of these diverse analyses of religion arises from a distinctive understanding of the dynamics of industrial society, and each of them departs significantly both from the classics and from Parsons's influential synthesis.

# 5
# Differentiation and its discontents

The idea that institutional differentiation has made religion problematic in advanced industrial societies has also been elaborated by scholars who do not necessarily share Luhmann's, Berger's, or Luckmann's assumptions. This chapter will be devoted to a discussion of theoretical positions which, in widely different ways, argue that religion is problematic either because industrial society is coming 'unglued' or because it is being excessively well integrated. There is general agreement among these scholars that religion's capacity to integrate societies by means of shared beliefs, values, motivations and sentiments has become irrelevant, marginal, or inadequate; but they reach different conclusions about the capacity of industrial societies to survive in the absence of such overarching symbols. At one extreme is the view that the stability and survival capacity of industrial society have been adversely affected by the decline of religion. But at the opposite extreme is the view that the peculiar situation of advanced industrial societies may actually create opportunities for new forms of religious expression.

The connection between a differentiation model of industrial society and religion has been most authoritatively articulated by Bryan Wilson in the form of a strong thesis about secularization:

> Secularization is associated with the structural differentiation of the social system – separation of different areas of social activity into more specialized forms . . . Instead of work activity, family life, education, religious practice, the operation of law and custom and recreation, all being part of each other and affecting everyone in more or less

self-sufficient close-knit small communities, as occurred in large measure in all pre-modern societies, we have highly specialized places, times, resources, and personnel involved in each of these areas of social life, and their efficiency and viability has depended on this process of specialization.

(Wilson, 1976, p. 40; cited in Bell, 1980, p. 328)

In fact, Wilson's preoccupation with secularization is largely driven by the belief that the decline of community, by definition, implies the decline of religion. Thus:

religion may be said to have its source in, and to draw its strength from, the community, the local, persisting relationships of the relatively stable group . . .

[W]hereas religion once entered into the very texture of community life, in modern society it operates only in interstitial places in the system . . . One might, then, juxtapose the two phenomena: the religious community and the secular society.

(1982, pp. 154–5)

He regards religion as 'the ideology of community' which has been marginalized by the integration of local communities into whole societies ('societalization'). There is allegedly no further need for religious ideology in increasingly rationalized societies in which integration and purpose are provided by the logic of rationality, function, system and utility. Consequently, Wilson contends that

Industrial society needs no local gods, or local saints; no local nostrums, remedies, or points of reference . . .

The large-scale societal system does not rely, or seeks not to rely, on a moral order, but rather, wherever possible, on technical order.

(Wilson, 1982, pp. 159 and 161)

In the few places where ideas of community persist, according to Wilson, they amount to nothing more than an outdated, sentimental rhetoric. Recourse to this rhetoric is said to be necessary only because we have no other language in which loyalties and goodwill can be summoned and expressed. But he regards the rhetoric as empty because it can no longer tap the shared moral values on which the legitimacy of social order supposedly depends. This enables the societal system to rely 'less on people being good (according to the lights of the local community), and more on their being calculable, according to the requirements of the developing rational order' (Wilson, 1982, p. 165).

Wilson acknowledges that religious activity is still lively in certain small groups, and this is consistent with his claim that secularization does not mean the demise of religion. He is, in fact, careful to apply the term 'secularization' only to the process whereby religion loses social significance, that is, it ceases to provide the major values, moral constraints and legitimation in society.

Now, the facts about the increasing rationalization, centralization and impersonalization of life in advanced industrial societies are barely disputable. But it is questionable whether the separation of religion from the apparatus of social control and legitimation necessarily means that religion's significance is in decline. It seems to me that Wilson's argument only succeeds if religion is equated with large religious organizations. Such an equation may well have appeared to make sense in, for example, Europe prior to the twentieth century or in parts of the USA today. But it is debatable whether large religious organizations are the sole 'habitat' of religion.

In my view, the connection between religion, obligatory beliefs and community may be an historical contingency. Religion has, in the past, been primarily associated with local communities for sound sociological reasons, but it does not follow that this is the only modality in which religion can operate or, indeed, has operated. There is a danger of mistaking historical contingency for categorical necessity. For, even by Wilson's own definition of religion as 'the invocation of the supernatural' (1982, p. 159), there is no *necessary* connection between religion and local community.

Further difficulties with the syndrome of declining community/societalization/differentiation/secularization have been raised by Daniel Bell (1980). The difficulties arise from (1) his particular conceptualization of 'religion', (2) his insistence on a conceptual distinction between culture and society and (3) his special understanding of the peculiarity of *post-industrial* society. The combination of these ideas enables Bell to conclude both that the concept of secularization is muddled and that religion has a future. These conclusions appear to be strongly at odds with those of the major exponents of secularization theory. Moreover, these conceptual disagreements are very revealing about some of the prevailing images of modern society as well as about the reasons why religion remains a problem for sociological analysis.

To begin with the conceptualization of religion, Bell is unusual among sociologists for emphasizing that religion is a 'set of coherent answers to the core existential questions that confront every group' (Bell, 1980, p. 333). He deliberately plays down the association with the supernatural, preferring, instead, to stress the claim that religion is one of the 'modalities of response by sentient men to the core questions that confront all human groups in the consciousness of existence' (ibid.). Religion is therefore conceived primarily as the search for unity of culture: not a matter of social relations. Consequently, Bell eschews the widespread practice of thinking about religion as a response to, or a reflection of, the social system. This is why he is impatient with schemes, like Wilson's, which tie religion to the structure of community. This is also why he categorically denies that the ground of religion is necessarily regulative, functional, or integrative for post-industrial society.

Secondly, Bell's emphasis on the narrowly cultural significance of religion as a response to existential predicaments is of a piece with his more general claim that, for the purposes of sociological analysis, culture and social relations should be kept separate. His argument is that, while societies are usually 'disjunctive' (contrary to the beliefs of Marxists and normative functionalists), the peculiar character of post-industrial societies is that they display a radical *antagonism* between the culture, the polity and the techno-economic realm. The nature, pace and direction of change in these three separate realms are also said to be different. These distinctions enable Bell to distinguish, further, between the secularization of the social system ('disengagement of religion from political life') and the profanation of culture (disenchantment and the emergence of an 'imperious self'). It follows for Bell that the shrinkage of the authority previously exercised by religious institutions is only half the story of modernity. The existential questions remain to be answered. Consequently, there will necessarily be new forms of religion (other than cultic crazes) which will 'return to the past to seek for tradition and to search for those threads which can give a person a set of ties that place him in the continuity of the dead and the living and those still to be born' (Bell, 1980, p. 349). Bell tentatively suggests that three new forms of religion will emerge in the West: moralizing, redemptive and mystical.

Thirdly, Bell's speculations about the future of religion must be set against the background of his highly distinctive image of post-industrial society. It centres on the idea that each of the three radically disjunctive realms which comprise modern societies has its own 'axial principle' and characteristic structure. Moreover, these principles and structures are not only in tension with each other but also contradictory. The orientation towards theoretical knowledge, efficiency and rationality in the typically bureaucratic structures of the techno-economic realm, for example, is said to be increasingly dominant over, and incompatible with, the orientation towards the norm of equality in politics and the norm of self-fulfilment in culture. Bell expects the three main realms to pull further apart from each other at the same time as the norms and structures of the techno-economic realm continue to strengthen their dominion over the other two. The new forms of religion are therefore depicted as reactions against the would-be hegemony of purely utilitarian norms and values. This clearly represents a marked departure from the Parsonian functionalists' model of industrial societies' normative integration as well as from Wilson's notion of societalization.

The main implication of Bell's thesis is that, while religious organizations have virtually vacated the realms of political power in post-industrial society, existential questions requiring religious answers still persist, and, as a result, new religious forms are likely to emerge. These forms are also likely to correspond with the contours of the social categories which will be crucial in a knowledge-based, service society. The problem for post-industrial society, in Bell's opinion, is that religious commitment is nowadays bound to be to sectarian groups and values rather than to society-wide, universal ideals. The tension between parochialism and cosmopolitanism is therefore regarded as a painful and unavoidable double-bind. But neither secularization nor profanation is regarded as inevitable.

Although Bell's thesis has the distinct merit of situating the dynamics of religion in the context of theoretical ideas about the transition from industrial to post-industrial society it can also be criticized for exaggerating the degree to which changes in religion can occur independently from changes in social structures (Wilson, 1979). It is also difficult to reconcile the claim that culture is a categorically separate realm of social life with the claim that the principles guiding the techno-economic structure have become dominant in the social system as a whole. The latter claim seems to contradict the former. Furthermore, it is not easy to infer from Bell's writings why he believes that the inner logic of culture has supposedly dictated a return to notions of the sacred at this particular historical juncture. In his eagerness to lay the ghost of normative functionalist reasoning about religion Bell appears to have erred in the direction of an exaggerated argument about cultural autonomy. An opportunity to develop a new sociological understanding of religion in post-industrial society may therefore have been compromised beyond repair.

But it should be added that many critics have also found serious fault with Bell's claims about post-industrial society. In particular, he has been criticized for exaggerating the extent to which increased reliance on theoretical knowledge, service industries and professional institutions represents a significant break with the trends long evident in industrial and capitalist society. The distribution of authority, power and life-chances, for example, does not appear to be sufficiently novel to warrant Bell's strong claims about the advent of a new form of society. In any case, as we shall see in Chapter 6, there are other ways of interpreting the meaning of the changes that have undoubtedly taken place in industrial societies in the mid-twentieth century.

A more moderate and less contradictory attempt to relate the future of religion to the development of highly differentiated industrial societies has been made by Richard Fenn (1970, 1972, 1978 and 1981). Like Luhmann, Luckmann, Wilson and Bell, he begins by acknowledging that the process of institutional differentiation has been crucial for advanced industrial society; and he rejects Talcott Parsons's belief that the relationships among social structure, culture and personality are mutually congruent and fundamentally guided by common values. But Fenn extends the argument about differentiation to the point of claiming that the process of differentiation has gone so far as to eliminate the possibility that social order could any longer be based on shared normative commitments. For him, there is no pattern of congruence between the norms guiding personality, culture and social structure: 'Religious values seem to have little *demonstrable* relationship to what people actually do in work and politics' (Fenn, 1972, p. 16, original emphasis). Nor can community generate cohesion in modern society. Social order is, rather, a product of the overlapping bonds between people having different values, different roles and different personalities. The result is that societies are integrated without being cohesive.

According to Fenn, individuals choose their own religious commitments in advanced industrial societies, but there is no justification for believing that, as a result, religion fulfils a function for the whole society. Instead, Fenn prefers to argue that technical discussions of priorities in public policy lie at the root of modern social order: not basic values. Indeed, he suggests that strong religious and moral motivations could actually be dysfunctional for a whole society if they raised unrealistic expectations of congruence between the private and public realms of social life. This is why he argues that quietistic and introversionist forms of personal religiosity are best adapted to the predominance of instrumental rationality in the world of work and politics. But he also insists that such 'partial' forms of religion or ideology could never fulfil the kind of functions that religion has traditionally fulfilled in most pre-industrial societies. 'Secularization does not drive religion from modern society, but rather fosters a type of religion which has no major functions for the *entire* society' (Fenn, 1972, p. 31, original emphasis).

This thesis is intriguingly illustrated and amplified in Fenn's studies of the secularization of language (1981, 1982 and 1987). The central idea is that advanced industrial societies provide very little scope for authoritative utterances which might avoid ambiguity and uncertainty. Saying things 'for real' is the exclusive prerogative of liturgies and other ritual settings, according to Fenn, but the critical and instrumental criteria of truth which apply in the life-world and in the world of work or formal organizations have gradually precluded the very possibility that even liturgical language could be taken seriously. All that is left is the possibility that personal authenticity might be accepted as evidence of a commitment to speak the truth. Fenn notes that 'Secular institutions have a way of reducing authoritative declarations to mere assertions of personal opinion in the court or in the classroom' (1981, p. xxxiv) and that, as a result, the power of the state goes virtually unchecked by the kind of 'prophetic' language which used to be rooted in tradition and guaranteed by the social bonds of community.

Fenn's argument about the secularization of language eventually leads to an observation about religion in modern societies which might be supported by a great many sociologists of religion, namely, that religion continues to exist on the margins of mainstream society; it does not actually disappear from secular society. But I must emphasize that Fenn, unlike some other sociologists, does not regard this marginal religion as a merely residual or accidental phenomenon. On the contrary, he argues that it is the very nature of secular society which generates what he calls 'the paradoxical revival of religion'. This is because the rules governing many secular contexts

impose severe limitations on speech-acts that direct and declare, reserving these acts of speech to those properly authorized and trained to pronounce, judge, evaluate,

order, direct, implore, beg or even persuasively to suggest. Some religious groups . . . flourish precisely because
they provide the unauthorized and untrained, the laity,
with opportunities to declare, pronounce and direct . . .
Religious groups with Pentecostal fervor and authority in
their acts of speech may indeed flourish precisely because
of the successful secularization of educational, economic, or
political institutions in modern societies . . . [Thus] secularization creates a demand for the kind of speech-acts reserved
only to elites in modern societies.

(Fenn, 1981, p. 119)

Fenn's argument is therefore very different from that of most
proponents of a secularization thesis not only for acknowledging the persistence of religion in secular society but also,
and much more importantly, for suggesting that secularization
stimulates a particular kind of religion which mirrors the spirit
of the times. This is significantly different from the more widely
held view that religion is either accidental or fundamentally at
odds with that spirit. More importantly, Fenn's focus on the
secularization of language enables him to raise novel questions
about the relative *power* of the agents of religious organizations
to make forceful declarations and to issue cogent directions in
non-religious settings.

The other side of this coin is no less interesting to Fenn,
namely, the steps taken by secular authorities to limit the scope
of performative utterances made in the name of religion. His
approach is therefore more combative, dialectical and subtle
than that of many other versions of the secularization thesis.
It recognizes that secularization is not simply a disembodied
process of change at the highest institutional levels but is also
a matter of practical conflict in mundane social settings such as
classrooms and courts of law. Thus, the 'location and scope of
the sacred depends on the relative success of religious groups
in pressing their own claims and views of reality' (Fenn, 1978,
p. xx). The introduction of a *political* dimension into the debate
about secularization is a welcome departure from the tendency
to regard it as an abstract process over which human agents
appear to have little or no influence.

In this respect, David Martin's (1978) theory of secularization also represents an attempt to reveal the political and frequently violent aspects of the social conflicts which have shaped the development of religious organizations in modern times. Compared with Fenn, however, Martin appears to be relatively more interested in the twists and turns of religious history and less interested in the underlying cultural processes whereby struggles over the boundaries between the sacred and the secular are conducted. By contrast, Hunter (1987) draws attention precisely to the processes whereby left-liberal religious élites have apparently adopted an adversarial political and moral stance towards many aspects of advanced industrial societies. They represent a declining proportion of the so-called knowledge class, but their prestige is still believed to confer on them the capacity to legitimate (or otherwise) social arrangements and cultural standards. Hunter (1987, p. 374) therefore regards religious élites as the 'religious arm of the knowledge sector' of advanced industrial societies because they have forged an alliance with the central intellectual élites and have become spokespersons for the dominant ethic of post-industrial ideology. Hunter's reasoning is highly questionable but it is at least concerned with the politics of religion in societies which have departed from the classical models of industrial society.

An important implication of Fenn's insight into the 'agonistic' aspect of secularization is that, as religion declines in significance, it is also said to become more controversial. This is especially evident in his argument against Bellah (1970) that the US civil religion cannot simply be understood as a set of symbols representing the underlying continuity and unity of US society. In Fenn's view, civil religion has to be conceptualized as an attempt to *define* US society in a particular fashion. The attempt meets with resistance and with requests for clarification as the suspicion grows that the would-be definition of the situation is in fact an inauthentic form of political manipulation. The ambiguity and disagreement are not mere mistakes or inaccuracies; they represent fundamental differences of perception and evaluation. Moreover, there is no neutral position from which adjudication of the differences could be made. Consequently, political struggle and ethical debate are no less inevitable in connection with civil religion than is intellectual discussion. It also follows for Fenn, *contra* Shils (1975), that charisma is no longer a powerful force which emanates from the centre of modern societies and integrates them on the basis of a diffuse respect for central authority. Rather, Fenn regards the rhetoric of charisma as merely another outdated expedient for producing the appearance of cohesion.

Furthermore, Fenn anticipates that the long-term effects of the secularization of language will be to undermine the credibility and authority of *all* institutions responsible for trying to articulate public ethics. This is because secularization 'heightens anxiety about the individual's place in society and history' and 'undermines the capacity of societies to maintain belief in a symbolic whole that incorporates and transcends the identities and interests of their component parts' (Fenn, 1978, p. 8). In other words, the blurring of the boundary between the sacred and the secular simultaneously removes certain restrictions from individuals *and* lifts the limits on what can be done to individuals in the name of collectivities such as the state, the political party, or a totalistic religious sect.

Fenn's account of secularization represents an advance on previous formulations for many reasons, not the least of which is his intention to articulate, rather than resolve, the ambiguities, tensions and disagreements between competing theses about the phenomenon. For present purposes, however, the most striking aspects of his work are twofold. First is the emphasis on the social processes in which the sacred, the secular and the boundaries between them are fought over. Instead of imposing restrictive definitions of the key terms, Fenn recognizes that their meanings are subject to continual discussion and struggle at the level of social actors, groups and institutions. Differentiation and societalization are therefore regarded as the backdrop to these struggles: not their immutable causes. This position permits considerably more flexibility of approach and interpretive detail than is found in many other accounts of secularization in terms of societal differentiation. Secondly, Fenn's approach refuses to separate religion from its social context in advanced industrial societies. His account of secularization therefore deals with many more things than the declining significance of religion in isolation. The conditions, processes and consequences of secularization are all rigorously related to other features of modernity. The conclusion is that, in advanced industrial societies, religion has become more problematic in terms of both political-ethical disputes and sociological interpretations.

A further reformulation of classical theories of industrial society, normative functionalist models of modernity and strong claims about the uniqueness of post-industrial society has been made by Roland Robertson (1985b) in his attempts to refocus the problematic of religion on what he calls 'the global circumstance'. This refers to the idea that the economic and political consolidation of a world-system of interrelated nation-states in the twentieth century has given rise for the first time to a recognition that the world is really becoming a single place. Robertson's argument implies, then, that the internal differentiation of societies has paradoxically created the conditions in which a kind of reintegration can take place at a transnational level. But his notion of globalization goes beyond the main point of so-called world-systems theory, namely, that the process of crystallization of a transnational economic system linking capitalist centres with colonized peripheries eventually undermined the power of medieval and early-modern transnational religious organizations. His contention is that the process was intimately associated with religious ideologies right from its beginnings in the sixteenth century and that the degree of political and economic integration in the world-system has now reached such high levels that new religious themes are being generated. In other words, the argument is that religion was never made irrelevant by the emerging world-system and is currently being revitalized, especially in transnational religious movements, precisely by the success of global integration.

The idea that the capitalist world-system has given rise to a consciousness of globalization with positive implications for religion has not yet been seriously tested: only illustrated. But the idea is at least congruent with other arguments about the growing currency of holistic imagery in new religious and healing movements (Beckford, 1984). And there are grounds for thinking that concerns with social justice, equality and moral integrity on a global scale have been in the forefront of movements to revitalize several world religions in the past few decades. Robertson's thesis therefore demands serious consideration as an attempt to move beyond conventional ideas about the differentiation of industrial society. Indeed, he has criticized such models for failing to take account of worldwide forces which are allegedly in process of transforming the development of advanced industrial and developing societies alike.

Robertson's criticism is directed specifically at the widespread assumption that the processes of institutional differentiation and societalization *within separate societies* have eclipsed the social bonds of community and have consequently eradicated the grounds for religion. Against this view, he argues that the crystallization of a capitalist world-system has actually created a new, i.e. global, level of communality which, in turn, is allegedly producing a freshly religious perspective on human existence. This conceptual criticism of the conventional model of modern societies is complemented by empirical observations on 'the virtually worldwide eruption of religious and quasi-religious concerns and themes' (Robertson and Chirico, 1985, p. 222) in recent years. Moreover, Robertson claims that, in addition to the religiosity generated by relations between states, another form of religious awareness has been induced by the intervention of separate states into 'telic' matters such as human rights, inequality, life-chances and quality of life. The common thread running through these matters is 'humanity', that is, a concern with the ultimate meaning of human existence which transcends involvement in particular social settings. This is expressed in discourse about the self: not, however, in imperious isolation but in relation to the whole of humanity.

The conjunction of the global circumstance with the involvement of states in matters concerned with the ends of humanity is responsible, according to Robertson, for much of the current revitalization of religion. This is another way of saying, with Fenn, that modern societies, far from dispensing with religion, actually generate religious impulses within themselves and in interactions among themselves. It is also a way of drawing attention to the increasingly controversial and conflictual character of relations between religious organizations and secular authorities in many parts of the world (Robbins and Robertson, 1987). Robertson's writings bring all of these concerns together in a comprehensive formulation of the sociological *and* social aspects of the problem of religion in modern societies:

> A pressure to connect religious and state domains in the modern world, regardless of the degree to which there is formal, constitutional separation, arises from the fact that increasingly we face the problem of the plurality of cultures and faiths at the global level. And that circumstance is almost certainly also a source for our own becoming more conscious of the 'deeper' aspects of modern life. By the same token, consciousness of roots, tradition, heritage, and so on, increases the likelihood that societies will draw upon religiocultural resources in defining their identities and that movements within and across societies will invoke religious symbols.
>
> (Robertson, 1987, p. 10)

The connection between religion and revolution in the modern world is central to this analysis of the shifting contribution of religion towards the distinctiveness of advanced industrial society.

All these variants on the idea that social differentiation has significantly modified the location, importance and power of religion in advanced industrial societies are based on the usually unstated premiss that pre-industrial societies tended to be relatively cohesive moral communities. They also seem to take for granted that religion symbolically represents this cohesiveness. Accordingly, evidence of social divisions or contradictions is taken to signify both a departure from the norm of a cohesive moral community and a problem for religion. As the next section of this chapter shows, however, the key problem of modern society has not always been identified with structural differentiation or the decline of normative regulation. Indeed, Michel Foucault has argued, admittedly with mixed results, that the individual in whom privatized religion is widely believed to be located nowadays is himself or herself a cultural artefact: not an unproblematic and universal component of the social world. Foucault's iconoclastic approach to the human sciences and, in particular, to their unexamined concepts of the individual person is therefore a useful vantage point from which to criticize some of the most deeply rooted assumptions of the sociology of religion.

DOMINATION AND ITS DISCONTENTS:
MICHEL FOUCAULT

Although Michel Foucault wrote relatively little about religion (Foucault, 1978, pp. 57–73; and 1982, pp. 208-16; Chidester, 1986), his proposals for 'general history', 'the history of the present' and the 'archaeology of knowledge' could have a strong bearing on ways of understanding the meaning of religion in the historical sequence of the allegedly discontinuous 'epistemes' or fields of systemic relations among hidden universes of discourse and discursive practices. In particular, Foucault's approach, by emphasizing the discontinuities between such epistemes as the Renaissance, the classical, the modern and the contemporary ages, relativized ways of thinking about secularization and especially the presumptions that this concept usually carries about the emergence of the supposedly autonomous individual of modernity. For, following Gramsci, Althusser and other structuralist theorists of culture and personality, Foucault regarded the notion of the individual as a construct of particular discourses, practices and apparatuses: not a naturally given basis or outcome of human development. In addition, he argued that knowledge about the individual 'subject' is related to societal structures of domination which reflect the differential distribution of power in society. He therefore characterized his work as a history of the various ways in which human beings have been transformed into subjects or, rather, objects.

There is an uneasy tension in Foucault's writings between the structuralist disposition to regard the relation between things and their signifiers as arbitrary and the Marxist practice of exposing the interests which allegedly make certain ideas legitimate or natural. Perhaps the best that can be said in his defence is that his understanding of 'interests' is much broader than that of most Marxists and is certainly not confined to a crude notion of social class. Instead, Foucault was prepared to find constellations of power relations in such specific social settings as the professions, the police, churches and social welfare agencies. He associated the growing power of these agencies with the production of ever more specialized knowledge which, in turn, has served to control more and more areas of so-called private life. The control is supposedly exercised by imposing categorizations and classifications which have the effect of inducing progressively sharper distinctions between acceptable and unacceptable notions of what a normal human individual is like.

The use of the sacrament of confession in the Roman Catholic Church, for example, was cited by Foucault (1978) as a practice which became adapted to the modern discourse of sexuality. It did not consign sex to the shadows but it compelled professionals and experts in many specialisms to speak about sex endlessly whilst, at the same time, insisting that it be kept a secret. Euphemisms, metaphors and sanitized analogies therefore cloaked the compulsory topic in mystery. Foucault believed that this combination of a compelling discourse with a secret subject-matter generated more and more opportunities and methods for the control of human beings. According to Foucault, this is a good example of the way in which people have learned to regard themselves as 'subjects' in the light of modern knowledge. In other words, the discourse of sexuality has transformed people into objects by individualizing them in particular ways.

Religion, as an institution and in the form of concrete groups and professional roles, interested Foucault mainly for the techniques that it allegedly supplied to the overall 'economy of power relations' – partly from the point of view of domination and partly from the point of view of struggle and resistance against domination. Thus, the Reformation represented a great crisis of the Western experience of subjectivity and a revolt against the kind of religious and moral power which gave form, during the Middle Ages, to this subjectivity. The need to take a direct part in spiritual life, in the work of salvation, in the truth which lies in the Book – all that was a struggle for a new subjectivity.

(Foucault, 1978, p. 213)

The ironic importance of this kind of struggle, for Foucault, was that it led to the eventual rise of the nation state as a novel complex of power relations. For the kind of 'pastoral power' that had previously been fostered by the major Christian churches was apparently assimilated by the post-Reformation states in such a way that religious techniques of individualization were combined with the political technique of totalization. The result, as Foucault argued in a thoroughly functionalist vein, was that the declining vitality of church organizations was accompanied by the diffusion of individualizing pastoral power throughout modern societies:

Power of a pastoral type, which over centuries – for more than a millennium – had been linked to a defined religious institution, suddenly spread out into the whole social body; it found support in a multitude of institutions. And, instead of pastoral power and a political power, more or less linked to each other, more or less rival, there was an individualizing 'tactic' which characterized a series of powers: those of the family, medicine, psychiatry, education, and employers.

(Foucault, 1982, p. 215)

The practical implication of Foucault's insight into the religious origins of the modern and contemporary epistemes is that

We have to imagine and build up what we could be to get rid of this kind of political 'double bind' which is the simultaneous individualization and totalization of modern power structures . . . We have to promote new forms of subjectivity through the refusal of this kind of individuality which has been imposed on us for several centuries.

(Foucault, 1982, p. 216)

This is the aspect of Foucault's work on which his critics are most divided. On the one hand, he is accused of describing the social world as so completely in the grip of total power that resistance is literally unthinkable. In other words, he is logically unable to present an alternative because he has already described the present system as one of total domination. But, on the other hand, it is said that his purpose was not to describe the present system as totally controlled or to propose alternatives: only to arouse a sense of such strong resentment in his readers that they would be inspired to criticize their own situation and, thereby, at least to try to mitigate the worst excesses of domination. It is an empirical question whether religion could serve as a source or medium of this type of immanent self-critique.

In some respects, Foucault's work seems to stand Weber's account of modernity on its head. Instead of positing rational individuals as the originators of a rationalized world, Foucault seems to posit structures of power as the originators of modern individuality. This is in accordance with the structuralist practice of de-centring the subject and of according priority to the interplay of structural components. It has the effect of casting modernity in a light which is very different from that cast by Weber – and, indeed, by Parsons and the subsequent theorists of rationalized modernity. It also casts an ironic shadow over the attempts by Berger and Luckmann to devise a phenomenological and interactional sociology of religion, for in Foucault's opinion analysis of the social production of meaning and identity is empty unless it is related to underlying relations of power. To say that humans generate *nomoi* and sacred *cosmoi* is only a small part of the task of a history of the present; the other, more important part is to decode those structures of meaning in terms of the shifting distribution of power and, even more importantly, to challenge and to change them. A further effect of Foucault's approach to the key problem of modernity is to call in question the assumption that human societies have ever been integrated on the basis of anything other than power. This means that communally based societies were never based primarily on normative consensus and that the prevailing notions of individuality tended to be moulded to suit the interests of the dominant powers. For Foucault, then, the main problem of modernity was not social differentiation, the decline of community, or the separation between public and private spheres. On the contrary, it was what he considered to be the dehumanizing power of the many institutions which elicited from individuals a pervasive sense of being subjects and of thereby being duped into conformity with ruling interests. The problem is therefore one of excessive integration or control. But Foucault did not regard this situation as a stage of an evolutionary process of development; it represented merely the contemporary expression of an immanent problem.

Yet, Foucault maintained a sceptical attitude towards all would-be universally valid schemes for diagnosing or remedying the problems of modernity, preferring, instead, to subject all forms of knowledge, discourse and social practice to an unrelenting criticism of their capacity to transform human beings into individualized subjects. As many critics have pointed out, however, Foucault's refusal to countenance theories which ground action in universal qualities seems to undermine the basis of his own critique.

Leaving aside the philosophical difficulties with Foucault's rejection of claims to the grounds of universal truth, it is clear that there is immense scope for the investigation of the individualizing and totalizing procedures of religious organizations and discourses. For, although Foucault may have correctly described the diffusion of 'pastoral power' across many non-religious institutions, it does not follow that religion has been deprived of all power. It is ironic that Foucault's project for a history of the present remained stalled at the medieval and Reformation periods as far as religion is concerned. But it would be well worthwhile to examine the interrelatedness of contemporary discourses about the self, the body, birth, death, illness, health and spiritual well-being. The religious input to these discourses is considerable, as it is to the discourses of human rights, justice and peace as well. Moreover, the practices of confession and testimony, in addition to being diffused throughout modern society, according to Foucault, are still central to the activities of many religious organizations.

Foucault's work deserves the serious attention of sociologists of religion for questioning the meaning of the term 'individual' especially as it tends to be used in those influential theories which locate religion in the private, as distinct from the public, sphere of modern societies. One of the effects of Foucault's radical approach is to show that this very distinction, which is widely employed in the social and human sciences, is itself a cultural product that is intimately tied to features of numerous modern discourses. To borrow a structuralist image, the distinction could be said to belong to the grammar of social relations and to take its significance from its relationships with other grammatical concepts. It has no independent meaning. Similarly, the meaning attributed to 'individual' is derived from particular cultural-historical contexts and cannot be identified separately from them. As a result, Foucault would presumably have been reluctant to accept the idea that, for example, personal meanings or values had been cut adrift from systems of public regulation in modern societies. In his view, the very meaning of the personal would have been generated by discourse about the public.

It would also have been difficult for Foucault to agree with the claim that the 'everyday management of the state and the surveillance of society' (Turner, 1983, p. 240) had only a marginal connection with religion. Indeed, the most provocative and disturbing aspect of Foucault's thought is the implication that the very idea of privatized religion, far from being marginal to the operation of modern society, might actually be a pre-condition for the latter's success. It would be thoroughly in keeping with his philosophical position for Foucault to have regarded the belief that private thoughts and feelings were marginal to the reproduction of societal domination as evidence that exactly the opposite was true, namely, that effective control and surveillance were conditional upon the belief that the individual could be considered as an autonomous monad.

In sum, Foucault's analyses of modernity suggest that sociologists of religion may have given so much attention to processes such as structural differentiation and the decline of community that they have neglected to explicate adequately the concept of the individual. The concept tends, as a consequence, to have purely residual value. Foucault's writings are a challenge to make better sociological sense of the interplay between notions of structure and notions of individuality.

In sum, the normative functionalist synthesis of classical sociological ideas about the meaning of religion in industrial society has been extensively modified and questioned since the 1960s. Some theorists have not seriously challenged the usefulness of the term 'industrial society', but others have found it necessary to introduce new characterizations such as post-industrial or global society. In any case, they are all roughly agreed on one thing: religion remains a challenging sociological problem in societies subject to processes of differentiation and rationalization. As we shall see in Chapter 6, however, there are still more reasons for regarding religion as an interesting sociological phenomenon in the late twentieth century.

# 6

# Ideology, new social movements and spirituality

## LATTER-DAY MARXISMS

One of the ironies of the modern sociology of religion is that, for all its dependence on 'classic' theories of industrial society, it has only rarely found explicit use for Marxist perspectives. Marxist sociologies of religion are virtually non-existent in the communities of English-speaking sociologists.[1] The reasons for this lacuna may be, as Marie Augusta Neal (1985, pp. 339–40) has argued, that topics for research are determined by the likelihood that they will attract funding. As Marxism is politically suspect in many quarters it is unlikely to figure prominently in applications for research grants. This may be true but it is only part of the story. A more important consideration is that the Marxist model of capitalist society may appear to 'explain away' religion as an epiphenomenon and would, therefore, be unlikely to be built into fundamental thinking about the functioning of religion in the modern world.

With the advent of various Marxist and quasi-Marxist theories about advanced industrial, post-industrial, or late capitalist society, however, there has been a small revival of interest in historical materialist analyses of religion. Roger O'Toole (1984, pp. 188–94) may have exaggerated the impact that this revival has had on the sociology of religion, but it cannot be denied that the *prospects* for a serious Marxist analysis of religion have improved in the last two decades (McLellan, 1987). What is more, some new Marxist perspectives on late capitalist society imply that religious issues are no longer entirely marginal or epiphenomenal.

In so far as Marxist or quasi-Marxist ideas have exerted any appreciable influence on the sociology of religion in recent years they originate from theoretical positions which move beyond the positivistic and reductionist elements in the thinking of Marx, Engels and most of their pre-Second World War commentators (Maduro, 1977). These new ideas demand our consideration because they indicate that the kind of problems bequeathed by the earliest forms of historical materialism are now being superseded in such a way as to suggest that, in late capitalist societies, religion may actually be more interesting to Marxists than it was thought to be in the old models of industrial society. There is also the suggestion that, as religious conflicts escalate in developing countries, a Marxist perspective becomes all the more appropriate (Maduro, 1982).

Structuralist and functionalist Marxisms, in particular, can be interpreted as responses both to the evident political failures of Western European Communist parties in the late 1950s and to the evident difficulties that Marxist theories faced in trying to account for many of the continuities and changes in the social structure of capitalist societies. The process of de-Stalinization left the political parties in disarray. Marxist social scientists were driven at the same time to find fresh ways of explaining such things as the relatively low levels of overt class conflict, the resilience of capitalist enterprises, the rise of an apparently new middle class and a privatized working class, the class identity of the growing number of employees in positions of managerial or technical authority, the status of women, the persistence of governing élites, the meaning of racial and ethnic conflict, the abiding phenomenon of working-class conservatism, the growth of a new international division of labour and the emergence of a world-system of nation states. In coming to grips with some of these phenomena Marxist scholars introduced novel concepts and perspectives which have cast religion and spiritual issues in a fresh light. These theoretical innovations will be discussed in this chapter in terms of the legacy of Antonio Gramsci, the influence of structuralism and the fascination with new social movements.

ANTONIO GRAMSCI AND THE 'NEW ORDER'
OF HISTORICAL MATERIALISM

In comparison with the above list of intellectual challenges facing Marxist social scientists after the Second World War, the phenomenon of religion was not widely considered to be either urgent or interesting. Scholars who persisted with Marxist studies of religion were mainly anthropologists and historians. But the gradual appearance in translation of Antonio Gramsci's writings in the 1950s and 1960s offered the first new direction for historical materialism's approach to a sociological understanding of religion and other aspects of ideology. This new direction represents a radical departure from the old problematic of base and superstructure; indeed, Gramsci could be said to have dissolved or bypassed this frequently taken-for-granted conceptual scheme by means of a radical shift of philosophical perspectives.

Part of the attraction of Gramsci's approach was its rejection of the positivistic and evolutionary excesses of both 'scientific' sociology and vulgar Marxism. His own view was that the subordinate position of the proletariat under conditions of capitalism was in process of becoming widely acknowledged among the mass of workers for what it was. In particular, Gramsci expected that the developing class consciousness of workers organized in workers' councils would lead to a form of political praxis which could usher in a socialist era. This expectation was part of his belief that 'scientific philosophy' should be rejected in favour of the notion that truth is relative to its historical situation. According to him, the truth of an idea can therefore only be assessed in terms of its acceptability in particular circumstances.

One effect of Gramsci's innovative epistemology was to dissolve or bypass the mechanistic distinction between material base and cultural superstructure; ideas were regarded as no less real than social relations and economic forces. He therefore defined praxis as an historically conditioned willingness to act in the light of current ideas and in the context of currently understood material circumstances. The most important implication of this idea for the sociological study of religion was that highly abstract generalizations were not to be trusted. Instead, the meaning of religion had to be decoded in terms of the real-life experiences of people at particular times and places. The conventional Marxist formula about the domination of material base over all cultural elements of the superstructure had no place in Gramsci's work.

The role that Gramsci attributed to intellectuals in his Marxist framework was also highly distinctive and is another reason for its current attractiveness to some sociologists of religion. In a Marxism that was largely stripped of economism and historical determinism intellectuals were encouraged to develop theoretical ideas in accordance with prevailing social and material conditions – but not in the abstract. The unity of theory and practice had to be maintained. In this way, the future could be *created* by praxis, provided that priority was given to action. Proletarian self-consciousness amounted to a form of praxis and was considered no less 'theoretical' than the theories of intellectuals. By the same token, the theoretical work of intellectuals was thought to be no less practical than the manual labour of proletarians. As a result, Gramsci took seriously the production and dissemination of religious ideas.

Gramsci used the historical record of the Roman Catholic Church as an important illustration of his argument about the role of intellectuals in developing praxis. His view was that the church had succeeded in shaping the minds of generations of its followers by striving to prevent a gap from developing between the formalized religion of its intellectuals and the popular religion of its uneducated masses in both rural and urban areas. This had been achieved partly by couching doctrine in the terms of popular culture. The lesson for communism, according to Gramsci, was partly that the working class needed its own 'organic' intellectuals to express the experience of the masses in their own language and, consequently, to shape their consciousness in the present and for the future. The lesson also implied that even an industrial working class displayed a religious 'potential' which, in the right circumstances, could underpin a new historical 'bloc' or alliance between peasants, workers and priests. For Gramsci, it was a matter of finding ways to express this potential which would not distort it by contamination with the ideology purveyed by the 'traditional' intellectuals of the church.

In general, Gramsci was contemptuous of what he considered to be the Catholic Church's ideological compromise with the state and the ruling groups of civil society. He also criticized the church's allegedly ruthless use of its organizational power to crush resistance and unauthorized innovation. Yet, he believed that it might be possible for the peasantry and the working class to resist the Catholic hegemony by cultivating a non-ecclesiastical form of religion which would be free from the ideological contamination of dominant class interests. He therefore looked to elements of popular culture and folklore to play an important role in guaranteeing both the 'organic' character of this would-be demotic religion and, in consequence, its opposition to the values of high culture. In this respect, Gramsci anticipated much of the interest that sociologists of religion show nowadays in popular, folk, customary, common, or diffused religion. But it should not be forgotten that his interest in this topic was strictly part of a much wider concern with the social and cultural conditions of a proletarian revolution. If there is nostalgia for the 'ages of faith' in Gramsci's writings it is undoubtedly tempered by his revolutionary aspirations.

Moreover, Gramsci's conceptualization of religion was so broad that it is virtually merged with 'ideology'. What religion and ideology had in common, according to Gramsci, was a powerful articulation between a general conception of the world and specific rules for conduct. This particular conceptualization is notably more inclusive than Marx's or Engels's formulations. It was therefore compatible with Gramsci's contention that religions are complex sets of beliefs and practices which have different functions and resonances for different social classes and class fractions at different times. Nevertheless, he clearly saw that the Catholic Church had always tried to impose unity on this complexity and variety by stressing allegedly timeless and universal categories and verities. This is the 'jesuitical' form of Christianity that he disparaged in comparison with the 'popular' forms which, according to Gramsci, had expressed the will of the peasantry and the working classes at certain historical junctures.

Control over consciousness by cultural means is what Gramsci meant by 'hegemony', and he regarded this as an essential pre-condition for the exercise of political power. The task of working-class intellectuals, according to his political programme, would be to popularize new cultural ideas (including the potential for a new spirituality) which would replace existing world-views and lay the foundation for a new social order. This involved a combined form of spiritual and social liberation at grass-roots level rather than a purely political seizure of power. But it had to be separated from the Catholic Church's official form of religion if it was to be an authentic expression of working-class experience and aspirations. In other words, it had to be revolutionary rather than passive or restorative.

Gramsci's version of historical materialism offered the advantage of retaining the conventionally Marxist emphasis on the connection between social classes and consciousness without, at the same time, reducing the connection to a matter of a mechanical 'reflection' or 'determination'. As a result, the question of the relative autonomy of religion does not really arise in the Gramscian perspective. This is because the distinction between the material base and cultural superstructure was softened in favour of the idea that even the most clearly 'material' forces have to be apprehended through cultural categories. The categories of base and superstructure were therefore dissolved into a unitary perspective which highlights both the ideational and material aspects of social struggles against alienation and oppression. Social change is understood to be the result of complex struggles between groups of human beings seeking to impose their meanings on the material, social and cultural aspects of life. No aspect is necessarily granted priority over the others. In reality, the outcome reflects both the strength of the 'will' to achieve emancipation from restraints that are defined as unacceptable *and* the strength of the social organization for mobilizing revolutionary consciousness. Ironically, Gramsci's relatively positive attitude towards religion in certain circumstances has met with considerable indifference among sociologists of religion outside Italy. But it has had an invigorating effect on current thinking about new social movements. The argument of a later section of this chapter will be that the sociology of religion could benefit from taking Gramsci and some quasi-Marxist students of social movements seriously.

Gramsci did not rule out, on purely philosophical grounds, the possibility that religion could serve as one of the vehicles of revolutionary class consciousness. Indeed, the parallels that he drew between some popular insurrectionary heresies of the Middle Ages and the idea of government by workers' councils indicated that he believed that religion could be a force for liberation in certain circumstances. In this respect, some of Gramsci's ideas have been formative for present-day Christian theologies of liberation. Moreover, the importance that he attributed to the role of intellectuals in shaping ideology eventually found an echo in the primacy that is commonly accorded nowadays to theoretical knowledge in various models of advanced industrial or post-industrial society. This is a further reason, then, for believing that the place of religion in modern societies will be of increasing interest to Marxist sociologists.

## STRUCTURALIST MARXISMS

In spite of Gramsci's achievements, many scholars continue to doubt whether modern Marxism is capable of producing fresh insights into religious phenomena. Some scholars have argued that, in any case, the thesis of relative autonomy, which had been employed by Engels, Bernstein and Kautsky to explain religion, would have to become increasingly eclectic if it was to survive at all. The problem was that the historical materialist model of relations between a materialist base and a cultural superstructure appeared to generate a sterile economistic reductionism. It is not surprising, then, that interest in the sociology of religion tended to be extremely low among Marxists but that when the interest of some of them revived in the 1960s it took the form of precisely the kind of eclecticism that had been expected, namely, structuralist or 'scientific' Marxism.

One of the many ironies about the relation between Marxism and religion is that the extensive dialogue between 'humanist' Marxists and Christians, existentialists and phenomenologists which took place mainly in France following the Second World

War gave rise to very few *sociological* studies of religion. The dialogue was largely confined to the levels of metaphysics and ecumenical tactics, on which sociological considerations seemed to have little bearing. By contrast, some of the self-proclaimed structuralist and 'scientific' Marxists, for whom dialogue with religionists held *no* interest, actually applied themselves to sociological analysis of religion. Structuralist Marxism's interest in religion has only rarely extended, however, to the religious practices, institutions and organizations of contemporary industrial societies. Rather, it tends to be narrowly focused on religion in *pre*-industrial or industrializing societies (see, e.g., Houtart, 1974).

What was the attraction of structuralism? It offered the advantage of overcoming to some extent the limitations of two components of classical Marxism: the mechanistic base/superstructure model and the empiricist thesis that consciousness either mirrors reality or is false. The advantage lay in recognizing that ideology (including religion) was not simply a reflection in the minds of individual actors of capitalist social relations but was an allegedly structural feature of all social formations. As such, ideology was believed to enjoy a certain degree of independence from the rest of society. That is, the *content* of ideology was considered to be relatively autonomous; but it was still the economic forces which determined 'in the last instance' whether, how and to what extent ideology would dominate any historical juncture. It was therefore believed that the ideological realm developed in different ways and at different rhythms from other parts of the social totality. This marked a significant departure from the more mechanistic and deterministic forms of Marxism which had tended to assume that social formations were unitary and tightly knit structures. Consequently, religion became a less threatening object for study because its persistence or vitality no longer represented such a grave theoretical problem. The connection between economic forces and cultural or social forms had been loosened to a considerable extent.

In trying to establish 'scientific' Marxism, and to distinguish it sharply from Hegelianism, Louis Althusser (1969) came to the forefront of an intellectual movement to make historical materialism more sensitive to the precise structures of relations between levels of the social whole. In particular, efforts were made to specify the ways in which the basic contradiction between capital and labour could be mediated by concrete historical circumstances reflecting political, ideological, cultural and religious conditions. The main implication for a Marxist sociology of religion was that religious phenomena, as ideology, could be taken seriously as one of the conditions of social order and change. That is, religion was considered capable of contributing relatively independently towards the accumulation of contradictions which were expected ultimately to precipitate social revolution. The ideological function of religion was therefore taken to be the provision of a mythical image of unitary social order which masked the underlying contradictions: 'The opacity of social structure makes necessarily *mythical* the representation of the world necessary for social cohesion' (Althusser, quoted in Larrain, 1979, p. 156, original emphasis).

Althusser's writings are focused mainly on France and, in so far as they touch on religion at all, on the Roman Catholic Church. He has shown little interest in comparative analysis of ideology, but others have applied his ideas to different societies and religions. Indeed, structuralist Marxism has probably been most enthusiastically applied by anthropologists to religion in pre-industrial societies. Godelier's (1977) studies of contemporary pre-industrial societies, for example, transposed the distinction between base and superstructure into a functionalist framework. The *substructural* or determining forces in any society were identified as those which functioned in order to ensure its continuing production and reproduction. The *superstructural* functions were defined as varied but essentially different from those of societal production and reproduction. Godelier believed that it was a matter of empirical research to discover precisely how the substructural and superstructural functions were fulfilled in any given society. The distinctiveness of the capitalist type of society was that economic forces were both determinant *and* dominant, i.e. the institution which fulfilled the substructural function was also dominant in the sense of actually controlling most social practices and beliefs. By contrast, Godelier's anthropological research provided examples of pre-capitalist societies in which religion, among other things, fulfilled substructural functions and was the dominant institution in the sense of setting limits to the relations between other institutions. (For criticism, see Terray, 1972, p. 143.)

On the one hand, then, structuralist Marxism attributed considerable independence to ideology (including religion), and this appeared to make religion a more interesting and important object of study. But, on the other, the pervasive functionalism of the Althusserian version of structuralist Marxism worked in the opposite direction. The category of religion was still consigned to the status of a mechanism for producing and maintaining the mythical cohesion of the social whole. Admittedly, Althusser, Godelier and their associates achieved a breakthrough in Marxist thinking by their refusal to conceptualize religion as a mere epiphenomenal reflection of social forces or as a figment of distorted consciousness alone. They recognized that religion, like all ideology, enjoyed an existence in its own right and was therefore as real as material forces. And their distinctive claim that ideology 'interpellates' the kind of subjects required by societies at particular stages of development represented a promising departure from many earlier, and more deterministic, forms of Marxist thinking about ideology. But it is difficult to deny that these innovations have merely shifted the location of determinism; they have not abolished it. The forces and social relations of production remain the ultimately determining element of the social totality. It may be conceptualized as a looser kind of structure than is common in more conventional Marxist models of society, but the totality is still endowed with the capacity, if not the requirement, to impose its interests on the components of the system. In other words, a 'hidden hand' still moves the system in a determinate direction, for religious ideology is believed to shape the prevailing sense of identity and subjectivity in accordance with the social class interests that are assumed to dominate the totality.

In the light of some of the criticisms that have been levelled at structuralist Marxism, attempts have been made to fashion a more acceptable historical materialist approach to understanding religion without necessarily abandoning the idea that ideology enjoys relative autonomy from the forces and social relations of production and is not to be equated with errors or false consciousness. In the first place, Turner (1983) and his associates (Abercrombie *et al.*, 1980 and 1986) have argued that the so-called dominant religious ideology of feudalism had the function less of keeping the peasantry in subordination to the material interests of landowning classes and more of preventing the ruling classes from abandoning their commitment to the conservation and legitimate transmission of family property across generations. This revisionist thesis departs even further from economistic Marxist assertions about the connection between material forces and ideology with the claim that, in the modern world, this connection is purely contingent. More specifically, 'In late capitalism, individual motivation does not require the sustenance of the Protestant Ethic' (Abercrombie *et al.*, 1986, p. 179). Much more important for the reproduction of the capitalist mode of production are said to be the various 'discourses' which give a particular identity and place to economic actors as individuals within hierarchical work organizations. The corollary of this view of late capitalism is that the mode of production no longer 'needs' the discipline and morality which had originally been supplied by the Christian religion. Secularization is therefore explained as a function of the changing nature of capitalism and of the corresponding growth of social control by means of bureaucracy, educational classification, work discipline, medical surveillance, social welfare and the mass media. The influence of Foucault's ideas is strong on this revisionist sociology of religion.

One effect of this reorientation of historical materialism has been to shift attention away from questions about the chronological aspects of the relation between ideas and social conditions. Instead, priority is given to the mechanisms by which ideological discourses are created, transmitted and appropriated – a loud echo of Gramsci's writings and a convenient bridge to studies of everyday or popular beliefs. It also reflects a conviction that capitalism and industrial society are not static, universally valid categories. They are said to have undergone extensive transformations especially in respect of the number of discourses that can be sustained in late capitalism or advanced industrial society.

This line of historical materialist analysis converges to some extent with Luckmann's phenomenological interpretation of the condition of modern religion. Preliminary insights into the family ethics of medieval Christianity, the institution of confession, the religious roots of individualism, the ideological function of mysticism and the significance of secularization for the bureaucratic surveillance of individual citizens (Turner, 1983) have already emerged from this refocused Marxism. But outstanding difficulties with its application concern the functionalist logic of its basic assumptions, the tendency to be selective about historical evidence, the willingness to be content with illustrating (rather than testing) its contentions and the danger of downplaying the extent to which people resist or refract the identities that ideological discourses may offer them.

A way of avoiding some of these difficulties without abandoning the key assumptions of historical materialism and structuralist sociology has been outlined by Kenneth Thompson (1986) and illustrated by reference to a number of ideological communities in Britain. He tries to combine Durkheim's sociological theory of collective representations with Althusser's theory of ideology into a unitary view of ideology as systems of representations in which 'people live their imaginary relations to the real conditions of existence' (Thompson, 1986, p. 24). But, in order to avoid functionalist reasoning and excessively abstract formulations, Thompson also insists that *any* part of culture could be considered ideological if it produced ideological effects, that is, if it persuaded people that their society is a particular kind of unitary place in which they have a particular kind of identity.

Thompson's eclectic conceptualization makes no a priori judgments about the conservative or radical character of ideological effects. This enables him to argue, therefore, that religion may at some times generate strongly conservative images of a society's would-be natural unity or cohesiveness and, at other times, elicit sharply radical responses to perceived oppression, alienation and resistance. Only sociological analyses of particular junctures could help to decode the ideological meaning of religious beliefs and practices. Even then, as his discussion of the competing interpretations of the history of bourgeois ideology and of the political incorporation of the working class in Britain in the nineteenth century indicates, it is unlikely that agreement would be reached among historians if more information were simply available. But Thompson is hopeful that comparison between ideological discourses in different societies might indicate the social and cultural factors which most heavily influence their effects. He shows, for example, that the discourse of religious pluralism in the United States has long been articulated with that of tolerance, ethnic differences and divine mission to the rest of the world. The ideological effect of bolstering social cohesiveness has also been reinforced by a discourse of scapegoating and boundary maintenance at times when threats were widely perceived to the nation's integrity. By comparison, different religious and political discourses have been articulated in Britain, but their ideological effects have been no less successful on occasion in shaping distinctive pictures of national or class communities.

Thompson is careful to deny, however, that there is any functional necessity for, or economistic determination of, these ideological discourses. They are not regarded as essential to the reproduction of the forces and social relations of production of capitalist or late-capitalist society, but their capacity to create and sustain 'ideological communities' is taken very seriously. In particular, Thompson emphasizes the power of complexes of articulated discourses to produce ideological effects. This is where a structuralist decoding of the 'grammar' of articulations between separate discourses becomes important, as Thompson shows in his maps of the changing connections between various religious, economic and political themes in both dominant and subordinate ideologies. In the spirit more of Gramsci and Foucault than of Althusser he denies (1) that these maps are necessarily tightly structured and (2) that there is a 'pure dominant ideology descending from above [or] a pure working-class ideology emanating from below'. Instead, he detects 'rather complex forms of interaction of political, cultural and ideological negotiation within and between classes' (Thompson, 1986, p. 79).

Starting from Gramsci's insights into the ideological importance of popular religion, Thompson proposes that even in late-capitalist society it is popular culture which brings the various discourses together in a loosely structured complex with ideological effects. The shift from religion to culture is not without its problems but may be justified in view of the fact that Gramsci's experience was very largely of the situation in Italy where the Roman Catholic Church was certainly hegemonic and crucial for all sectors of society. It is debatable, however, whether popular religion has ever enjoyed a similar degree of power in other capitalist countries. Nevertheless, Thompson shows that the religious components of popular culture are at least worthy of study for what they reveal about the practical struggles for control of the ideological field. Again, he makes the point that the ideological effects of popular religion and popular culture are not a priori conservative or radical. Much depends on the uses to which they are put by competing classes and interest groups.

Maduro (1982) makes very similar points about the articulations between religious and political struggle in developing countries. He argues that, in situations where religion remains a dominant institution, it would be impossible to develop strategies for social liberation without some kind of religious mediation. Religious change is therefore regarded as a pre-condition for social transformation. But it would also be necessary in these circumstances for a breach to take place in the exercise of traditional religious authority, either as a result of the internal reorientation of a religious organization or following a schism. Furthermore, even in cases in which religion is not a dominant institution Maduro believes that oppressed groups could still make use of religious symbolism in raising their class consciousness – providing that they first transformed their religious world-view into a more dynamic, liberating outlook. Finally:

> When all other socially possible forms of protest against economic, political, cultural, or other forms of domination are blocked by central power, as today in El Salvador, Guatemala, Chile, Argentina, and so on, the likelihood increases that the discontent of their subordinate classes may invade the church, and find religious expression in this church.
>
> (Maduro, 1982, p. 143)

This is all the more likely to happen, according to Maduro, if priests become what Gramsci termed 'organic intellectuals' or, in Bourdieu's (1971) terms, 'prophets' who make political interventions on behalf of subordinate groups.

Houtart and Lemercinier (1983), by contrast, claim that a new religious consciousness is in process of emerging among the oppressed social classes of Central America without the mediation of Catholic priests. Using insights from structuralist Marxism, they argue that a new form of popular religious consciousness has developed among the disadvantaged and that it turns biblical history into 'the history of people led by God in His process of liberation. Today, the people of God are all those who are oppressed, and the God who is alive in their midst is He who struggles alongside the people in their own struggle for a greater measure of humanity' (Houtart and Lemercinier, 1983, p. 172, trans. J.A.B.). Similar conclusions have also been reached by Opazo Bernales (1983) and Prendes (1983).

In addition to the epistemological 'loosening up' of Marxist sociology at the hands of structuralists and to the radical recasting of certain basic categories of historical materialism inspired by Gramsci, other innovations in Marxism and quasi-Marxism have also had implications for the understanding of religion. As we shall see in the next section, the most distinctive feature of these other innovations is that they have emerged from relatively new Marxist models of late capitalism or post-industrial society. The innovations are not so much corrections of analytical shortcomings as propositions about a *new* social reality. Moreover, they are not designed specifically to make better sense of religion. They merely have implications which *could* cast religion in a fresh and more challenging light.

## NEW SOCIAL MOVEMENTS AND RELIGION

Many sociologists have theorized about the nature of advanced industrial societies and their analogues such as post-industrial, late-capitalist or post-modern society. This section considers a set of ideas which have major implications for the way in which religion can be understood in these allegedly distinctive forms of society. The ideas are associated with various Marxist and quasi-Marxist scholars, none of whom can be considered as a sociologist of religion. What these scholars have in common is the belief that, as a result of basic transformations in the structure of capitalist societies entering the late, advanced or post-industrial stage, 'new' social movements (NSMs) have acquired major importance. Alberto Melucci (1985, p. 789) is representative of this belief: '[C]ollective action is shifting more and more from the "political" form which was common to traditional opposition movements in Western societies, to a cultural ground.' This means that, whereas the dominant conflicts of industrial society were supposed to have arisen from the contradictions between capital and labour, it is now believed that capitalism has undergone such major transformations that the site of the dominant social conflicts has now shifted to struggles over the quality of life and the desired shape of society in the future. Consequently, NSMs can be defined as forms of collective action and sentiment which are based on feelings of solidarity and which engage in conflict in order to break the *meanings* of the system of social relations in which they operate. The old system is being replaced, according to Melucci, with 'alternative codes': not with a new system of production or distribution.

Why the shift to *cultural* conflicts? The answer is in two parts. First, post-industrial or late-capitalist societies are said to be no longer founded on a purely 'economic' base. The production and distribution of goods are increasingly achieved, according to this view, by means of informational systems which are designed to ensure that markets and resources are efficiently exploited. According to André Gorz (1982, p. 105), '[W]ork linked to the administration and reproduction of social relations has grown more rapidly than work directly linked to material production, and has become a precondition of its heightened efficacy.' As a result, the old struggles for working-class participation in the system (citizenship) and for minimal standards of living (labour movement) are said to have been superseded by new struggles over the meaning and value of the social process as a whole (new social movements).

Secondly, whereas the class conflicts and the party political conflicts of industrial society were necessarily fought in symbolic media and were therefore partly cultural, the new movements are *primarily and directly* cultural. That is, they are less in the nature of demands for an improvement of material or political conditions and more like demands for a reinterpretation of the meaning of production and the orientation of society. Melucci even claims that NSMs have a *prophetic* function which goes well beyond the scope of movements for economic or political reform. 'They practice in the present the change they are struggling for: they redefine the meaning of social action for the whole society' (Melucci, 1985, p. 801) In this sense, much of the language of NSMs might be considered 'religious' by, e.g., Richard Fenn (1981, p. 98), for whom ' "prophetic" religious language is eventful, i.e., it brings about, re-creates and expresses the reality to which it refers'. By contrast, words in everyday life are not eventful; they are 'mere words'. Religious speech makes things happen or fulfils them. The same could be said about the illocutionary or operative force of the language widely used in some NSMs.

I shall examine three contributions to the quasi-Marxist debate about NSMs. The aim is to tease out some of the ways in which they make the meaning of religion in advanced industrial or late-capitalist societies more problematic than it appears to be in conventional Marxist accounts of industrial society.

*Jürgen Habermas*
The need to acknowledge the distinctiveness of the structures, processes and problems of late capitalism is apparent in many of the recent writings of Jürgen Habermas. He believes that a narrow analysis of the commodity form and of its articulation with the capital/labour relation, in accordance with Marx's theory of value, is no longer an adequate basis for understanding the kind of capitalism which has developed since the Second World War. Instead, he argues that the dominance of functional differentiation and *rationality* at the level of social systems, especially in the form of the principal media of exchange, namely, money and power, is now the driving force of social change and the source of the major social problems of modernity. He therefore regards studies of commodification, alienation and bureaucratization as

useful but one-sided; these unquestionably modern phenomena are merely symptoms of a more fundamental pathology of late-capitalist societies. Habermas's own theory is more complex than that of Marx or Weber and is based on the premiss that the social system has been uncoupled from the life-world.

The starting-point for Habermas's analysis of modernity is a distinction between the level of the social system and the level of the life-world. The latter is understood by Habermas as the repository of shared meanings which enable human beings to communicate with each other on a largely taken-for-granted basis and, thereby, to reproduce their social institutions and practices in both public and private spheres. The life-world refers to the domain in which socialization, legitimation and negotiation all take place. It is also the 'place' where communicative action occurs as people negotiate definitions of the situation. Habermas defines the social system, by contrast, as those increasingly extensive areas of life dominated by the pursuit of growth through money and power. These two 'steering media' are conceptualized as external forces which follow their own logic and are relatively unresponsive to the meanings and values generated in the life-world. In fact, Habermas believes that the logic of growth-for-its-own-sake, which governs the social system in late capitalism, is being foisted on to sectors of the life-world in the form of reifications. In this way, the particular logic of the social system takes on the appearance of natural or universal truth.

Habermas uses the distinction between social system imperatives and the communicative action of the life-world for two purposes. The first is to show that the logics of money and power are threatening to expunge the traces of ordinary human reason. And the second is to argue that ordinary human reason still amounts to a relatively autonomous resource which *could* be deployed in the criticism and repair of the social system. This is why he distances himself from the cultural pessimism of post-modernism and from the cultural traditionalism of neo-conservatives. Habermas wishes to preserve and extend the benefits of rationality and modernity, providing that they are subject to constant criticism and negotiation.

Unlike Weber and most of Habermas's colleagues in the Frankfurt School, Habermas claims that the development of reason in the life-world preceded the rationalization of modern social systems and that the rationality of actors therefore represents an important source of cultural opposition to these rationalized systems. This distinction was allegedly obscured by Marx's assumption that the development of the capitalist system had necessarily transformed the life-world as well as the spheres of production and distribution. As a result, Marx apparently failed to perceive that *'every* modern society, whatever its class structure, has to exhibit a high degree of structural differentiation' (Habermas, 1987, p. 340). Moreover, Marx's understanding of alienation allegedly arose from opposition to an inappropriately romantic ideal of life in pre-capitalist conditions and, consequently, could not be distinguished from the effects of structural differentiation in the life-world. Habermas's third reason for criticizing Marx's theory of value as an explanation of late capitalism is that it is based on an excessively narrow, instrumental model of the worker's purposive rationality. The model is therefore said to do insufficient justice to the reifications that take place in contexts other than that of wage labour, especially in the public domain.

The social system/life-world distinction also enables Habermas to argue that in late capitalism the relationship between them is necessarily paradoxical. Thus:

> The propelling mechanism of the economic system has to be kept as free as possible from life-world restrictions as well as from the demands for legitimation directed to the administrative system. The internal systemic logic of capitalism can be rendered in socio-theoretical terms by the formula that the functional necessities of systematically integrated domains of action shall be met, if need be, even at the cost of *technicizing* the life-world.
>
> (Habermas, 1987, p. 345)

The growing autonomy of the capitalist market and the bureaucratic state is said to be actually facilitated by norms and values generated in the private sphere; and it is in the interest of power and money for those same norms and values to be engineered. This process is part of the 'colonization of the life-world' whereby, according to Habermas, the principles on which the social system is integrated are imposed on the life-world. As a result, areas of life which had formerly been governed by norms and values generated in everyday social interaction and communication are progressively subjected to principles and criteria originating in the rationalized social system. For example, the application of formal, legal rules to relations between family members is said to reflect the paradoxical fact that the welfare state's attempts to cushion citizens against the worst aspects of inequalities and disabilities actually result in an even greater reduction of personal liberties:

> The more the welfare state goes beyond pacifying the class conflict lodged in the sphere of production and spreads a net of client relationships over private spheres of life, the stronger are the anticipated pathological side-effects of a juridification that entails both a bureaucratization and a monetarization of core areas in the life-world.
>
> (Habermas, 1987, p. 364)

The uncoupling of the social system and the life-world, according to Habermas, allows the former to develop in accordance with its own autonomous logic *and* to impose its principles and criteria on the latter with pathological effects. Habermas's particular fear is that the monetarization and bureaucratization of the life-world will eventually fragment it and prevent it from accomplishing the tasks of cultural and social reproduction. At that point, stability and continuity would become impossible. Social system integration would have been achieved at the expense of social integration.

It follows that movements of *cultural* protest and rebellion against various forms of reified rationality in the social system and life-world are of greater interest to Habermas than are the social movements which, according to him, used to be central to industrial society such as labour movements and class-based political parties: 'the new conflicts are not ignited by distribution problems but by questions having to do with the grammar of forms of life' (Habermas, 1987, p. 392). The underlying premiss seems to be that structurally induced class conflicts have been transposed into primarily psychological forms of expression which, in turn, shape the main cultural conflicts. In other words, capital/labour contradictions have allegedly been replaced by contradictions between, on the one hand, the increasingly heavy reliance of the state and other large organizations on justification for their activities in terms of efficiency and productivity and, on the other hand, the growing need for more substantive values on which to base a defence of societal integrity and harmony. This is said to provoke a crisis of legitimation which, in turn, is explained in terms of the structural incompatibility between instrumental rationality at the social system level and the intensified need for social integration at the life-world level.

In Habermas's view NSMs (primarily for peace, ecology, feminism and alternative technology) strive to prevent the erosion of areas of the life-world by reified rationality and to invest them with meanings which supersede the values of efficiency and productivity demanded by late capitalism as a system. This is their 'emancipatory interest', although it has to be said that Habermas is notoriously vague about the meaning of 'emancipation' in late capitalism. But what is clear is that he distinguishes between the potential for emancipation and the potential for resistance and withdrawal. Movements which seek only to resist and withdraw, according to Habermas, 'aim at stemming formally organized domains of action for the sake of communicatively structured domains, *and not at conquering new territory*' (Habermas, 1987, p. 393, my emphasis). Moreover, the 'resistance' movements are also divided into two types: (1) those which defend traditional practices and social ranking based on property ownership, and (2) those which employ human reason to work out 'new ways of cooperating and living together' (1987, p. 394). The first type includes middle-class protest movements against threats to residential neighbourhoods or higher taxation, as well as movements for regional or national autonomy. The second type has the capacity to resist tendencies towards colonization of the life-world on several levels: (1) the organic foundations of the life-world (pollution, pharmaceutical side-effects, despoliation of the environment); (2) problems of excessive complexity (mass famine, overpopulation, centralized control over data about private citizens); and (3) overburdening the communications infrastructure (search for communal identity on the basis of such ascriptive criteria as gender, skin colour, locality).

By comparison, it seems that the feminist movement is the sole representative of emancipation in Habermas's scheme. It is said to have 'the impetus of an offensive movement' (1987, p. 393) because of its struggle against patriarchal oppression and its determination to realize the promises anchored in universalist ethics and law. Instead of simply defending areas of the life-world from external threat, then, feminism impresses Habermas for extending the remit of critical reason into areas which had previously been in the thrall of irrational tradition and prejudices.

Emancipation therefore means something different from, and additional to, freedom from class exploitation. It involves the opportunity to exercise critical reason in the dialectical and unceasing process of rooting out reifications in social life. The 'ideal speech situation', in Habermas's terms, embodies the kind of presuppositions that are considered essential for the process of emancipation through critical reason. This is because it presupposes a kind of democratic *telos* of mutual understanding. Each participant has the opportunity to challenge every other participant's truth claims and criteria for validity and, in turn, to be challenged himself or herself. The ideal speech situation is also based on the assumption that all are oriented towards the collective good.

The significance that Habermas claims for NSMs in late-capitalist societies derives, then, from their explicit concern with the 'grammar of forms of life', that is, their distinctive type of critical discourse which aims to generate and to monitor consensual norms and values. He believes that this activity has become critical for late-capitalist societies because the very success of their predecessor, industrial society, has created problems for which they can offer no solution. According to Habermas, the problems of late capitalism and of the state have been displaced into the realms of socialization, education and morality. This is why he attributes so much importance to social movements concerned with the physical environment, nuclear power, gender relations, ethnic relations, peace and human rights.

If these movements really do rewrite the grammar of forms of life, there seems to be a case for arguing that they are doing something that religious organizations and movements have usually striven to accomplish. They are trying to disclose the ultimate significance of things – but not by means of revelation or deduction from fundamental principles. The process of critical reasoning appears to be an open-ended induction from agreed positions to ever more abstract levels of agreement and vice versa in a dialectical pattern.

In hinting at a broadly spiritual solution to the spiritual dimension of late capitalism's problems, Habermas is departing from the pattern established by at least two of his predecessors at Frankfurt, namely, Theodor Adorno and Herbert Marcuse. They believed that religion had become part of the total ideology of modern societies and was therefore an integral part of the logic of oppression, exploitation and suffering which supposedly sustains capitalism. By contrast, another of Habermas's predecessors, Max Horkheimer, persisted in the conviction that the utopian aspects of religion remained essential to the very possibility of a just society. Although he admittedly saw no place for dogmatic, church-oriented religion in late capitalism, Horkheimer was nevertheless convinced that a fundamentally religious sense of reciprocity and solidarity among human beings was indispensable to social life.

It is this particular line of Critical Theory that Habermas has extended into his own distinctive critique of the differentiated social system and into his unusual and guarded support for a humanistic kind of religion which might have emancipatory effects. Religion would be emancipatory in Habermas's opinion if it served as a vehicle of critical self-reflection and if, as a result of the process of secularization, it became separated from dominant interests. Indeed, Habermas implies that religious themes will become increasingly central to thinking about the emergent global society, particularly in connection with the search for a genuinely universalist ethics.

The 'window' that Habermas opens for a specific kind of religious and spiritual input into the critique of late capitalism is admittedly small in itself and even smaller in comparison with the opportunities for other kinds of cultural and political critiques. But for present purposes Habermas's ideas are significant because they represent a departure from several other sociological perspectives on the place of religion in the modern world. He clearly departs from conventional Marxist models of the base/superstructure model of social formations; and his defence of the power of critical reason is hard to reconcile with structuralist Marxism's strictures on ideology. At the same time, Habermas is critical of Weber's belief that the process of rationalization affected the social system and the beleaguered life-world equally. While he is therefore content with Weber's analysis of bureaucratization and state formation he also wants to mark off the life-world as a sphere of communicative action guided by a form of reason other than the narrowly instrumental. 'The communicative rationality of cultural modernity' (1987, p. 396) is not to be confused with the 'functionalist rationality' of the self-maintaining social system. This leaves open the prospect that disenchantment may not have destroyed the human capacity for self-critical reasoning. For the same reason, Habermas rejects Parsons's depiction of the modern social system as a unitary formation guided by a single set of values. The social system/life-world distinction is again employed as a means of keeping the unquestioned differentiation of the major sub-systems of the economy and the polity relatively separate for analytical purposes from the matter of the beleaguered life-world's survival. By the same token, Habermas would probably be critical of those theoretical schemes which regard social differentiation and societalization as fatal for the prospects of meaning formation and identity formation in anything other than a strictly privatized mode. Against Luhmann, Berger, Luckmann and

Wilson, for example, Habermas would presumably argue that there is no necessary homology or causal relationship between the rationalization of the social system and the evolution of human self-reflexive reason. He therefore holds out the hope of a strictly *collective* resolution, through communicative action, of late capitalism's major problems. The notion of privatized religious themes would not make sense from his point of view. But Habermas appears to accept the possibility that, in late capitalism, there may be an unexpected role for the religious themes that are nested in new social movements.

## Claus Offe

A similar attempt to move beyond Marx's characterization of industrial society in order to take explicit account of the new problems of late capitalism has been made by Claus Offe. Again, this updated Marxist approach has implications for the sociological understanding of modern religious phenomena, although sociologists of religion have been slow to take them up. This is more understandable than in the case of Habermas because Offe's writings appear on the surface to be dismissive of religion.

Like Habermas, Offe argues that the contradiction between labour and capital is no longer the central social conflict of Western societies. It has been pushed to one side by developments in the international division of labour, corporatism, the growing strength (and instability) of the state and the political co-optation of the working class. But Offe goes further than Habermas in arguing that the relationship of mutual dependence between capitalism and the Western welfare states is doomed to failure. The main reason given for this is the contradiction between, on the one hand, the welfare state's readiness to soften the hardships experienced by the working class in times of recession and, on the other, the declining capacity of capitalist economies to finance the increasing burden of welfare costs. A secondary contradiction is between the reformist ideology of the welfare state and the values which sustain the kind of relentless pursuit of capital accumulation that is believed by some to be essential for the success of capitalism. According to Offe, the latter contradiction feeds into a legitimation deficit; there is nothing in the values motivating capitalist accumulation which could legitimate the massive social expenditures of the welfare state. Conversely, there is nothing in the values underlying state welfare to support the unbridled pursuit of capital accumulation.

Offe shares some of Habermas's impatience with the old-style Marxism as well as with pre-war Critical Theory for attributing the failure of revolutionary socialism to such 'superstructural' obstacles as mass culture, tradition, or religion. Instead, Offe draws attention to the need to take account of state intervention in crises of late capitalism. He argues that the welfare state deliberately intervenes in order to preserve harmony between the economic, political and cultural spheres. In other words, the state actively provides explanations of problems and motives for action. According to Offe, late-capitalist societies are so complex, mobile and segmented that the family, the community and religious organizations are unable to supply adequate explanations and support. Moreover, he regards socialization as now largely the preserve of the state. It is allegedly accomplished by means of, *inter alia*, education, welfare agencies and the subsidized arts.

In addition, Offe believes that there is an increasingly sophisticated apparatus for the control or repair of deviance, dissidence, or disorder:

> Activities relating to eating, sexuality, health and disease cease to be governed by traditional cultural norms and are increasingly taught and controlled by the state . . . Nutritional and physical education schemes are complemented by a whole range of programmes of behaviour control – from campaigns against smoking and drinking to sex and drivers' education.
>
> (Offe, 1984, p. 277)

Matters are aggravated by the imposition of laws which are designed to 'invade the life-world of people' (1984, p. 281) and formally to regulate some of life's most intimate and emotionally charged experiences such as divorce, child custody, the limits of responsibility for elderly relatives and the determination of life or death, etc.

As late-capitalist societies become more complex, Offe argues, they also become more vulnerable, and this is why legal controls are imposed. But at the same time, *resistance* to state control increases, and this is why the tentacles of control have to be extended further and further, in a vicious circle, into areas of potential threat to state power. But the challenge to state power is no longer based on economic grounds. It has cultural roots and is articulated by new social movements which

> are to a significant extent non-economic; in the sense that they cannot be satisfied through distributive and productive means; they are concerned less with the quantity of income and wealth than with the quality of the natural and social conditions of life.
>
> (Offe, 1984, p. 293)

This is reminiscent of a point made by Habermas:

> The new conflicts are not sparked by *problems of distribution*, but concern the *grammar of forms of* life . . . [They arise from] the tangible destruction of the urban environment, the destruction of the countryside by bad residential planning, industrialization and pollution, health impairments due to side effects of civilization-destruction, pharmaceutical practices and so forth. They are developments that visibly attack the *organic foundations of the life-world* and make one drastically conscious of criteria of livability, of inflexible limits to the deprivation of sensual-aesthetic background needs.
>
> (1981, pp. 33 and 35 original emphasis)

In fact, Habermas (1981, p. 36) has gone even further in suggesting that the movement of resistance to the 'colonization of the life-world' is taking on distinctive characteristics:

An obvious component of the psychology movement and renewed religious fundamentalism and a motivating force behind most of the alternative projects and many citizens' action groups is the pain of withdrawal symptoms in a culturally impoverished and unilaterally rationalized praxis of everyday life. Thus, ascribed characteristics such as sex, age, skin color, even neighborhood and religion, contribute to the establishment and delimitation of communities, the creation of sub-culturally protected communications groups which further the search for personal and collective identity. High value is placed on the particular, the provincial, small social spaces, decentralized forms of interaction and de-specialized activities, simple interaction and non-differentiated public spheres. This is all intended to promote the revitalization of buried possibilities for expression and communication.

Incidentally, one of the interesting things about this characterization is that it depicts many of the features often attributed to 'privatized' or 'invisible' religion. But the reasons given for the NSMs are vastly different from those given by, e.g., Luckmann or Berger. The 'turn inwards' is not seen as a functional adaptation to increasing complexity. Rather, it is interpreted as a creative and, above all, critical challenge to a new order of control and exploitation.

Unlike Habermas, however, Offe deliberately excludes 'religious sects' from the category of NSMs on the grounds that they allegedly 'do not intend to win the recognition of their specific values and concerns as binding for the wider community' (1985, p. 827). In other words, they are particularistic and inward-looking. Offe may be mistaken, but this is, in any case, irrelevant to his argument about the themes and values of NSMs, namely, 'autonomy and identity . . . and opposition to manipulation, control, dependence, bureaucratization, regulation, etc.' (Offe, 1985, p. 829). It seems to me that these themes have a religious quality in so far as they have to do with the values that are considered ultimately important for human life and which transcend any particular social arrangements. They can also be considered fundamentally constitutive of human solidarities and therefore of collective will. They have to do with the determination to create a new form of society which would not be integrated on the basis of material gain and political power. This all comes close to aspects of at least two of the 'classical' conceptualizations of religion, namely, the emphasis that Durkheim placed on the celebration of social solidarity and the significance that Simmel attached to the unstated assumptions of trust and reciprocity underlying all collective action and sentiment. Offe unwittingly and perhaps unwillingly provides good grounds, then, for drawing attention to the religious quality of NSMs. At the very least, his discussion of NSMs illustrates the difficulty of distinguishing between religion and non-religion in the modern world as well as in modern sociology.

### Alain Touraine

Another quasi-Marxist who also explicitly excludes religious movements from the category of NSMs but whose analysis of social change nevertheless appears to touch indirectly on matters of religion is Alain Touraine. He has been responsible for empirical studies of many modern social movements: regional autonomy, Solidarity, the May Movement of students and workers in 1968, feminism, linguistic minorities and the anti-nuclear movement. In fact, he has directed an ambitious research project which is based on his controversial method of 'sociological intervention', the aim of which seems to be to open social movement participants' eyes to the wider theoretical significance of their practical activity and thereby to catalyse the movements' potential for creating a new type of society. This is all part of Touraine's long-standing criticism of sociologies which merely interpret human action as a conditioned response to external forces. His notion of the self-production of society is intended to counter sociological determinism with the claim that human beings make their own societies, including both repression and resistance. They have the choice, although it is, of course, framed by circumstances. Touraine's model of societies turns, therefore, on the idea that social process is *normally* a matter of struggles and conflicts over various stakes. *The* social movement is not conceptualized therefore as a marginal departure from society's normal structure; it is regarded as central to the very structure of post-industrial society. Touraine's (1985a, p. 91) argument is that the distinctiveness of social movements has hitherto been obscured by both the evolutionist tendencies of classical sociological theory and the functionalist leanings of modern theory.

Amidst all the struggles and conflicts over particular objectives such as tax reductions, capital punishment, antipornography, or anti-vivisection, Touraine has consistently tried to separate out a category of more basic tendencies: *the* social movement. What is at stake here is 'social control of the main cultural patterns' (Touraine, 1985b, p. 754), that is, the principles which govern what is to count as truth, production and morality. This overall social movement is said to be reflected to varying degrees in particular conflicts ('specific "fronts" of a general war': 1985b, p. 773). These conflicts may have three premature outcomes. They may (1) remain narrowly instrumental in aims, (2) develop into totalitarian institutions, or (3) become the basis of separate communities or states. Touraine considers all these outcomes as diversions of the social movement into premature termini. His aim, by contrast, is to keep the social movement free from such temptations of closure so that it may focus clearly on the central issue of deciding what kind of society would be most resistant to the forms of domination which are allegedly specific to *post-industrial* societies.

It is clear, then, that Touraine's concept of 'the social movement' is considerably more abstract than that of 'social movement organization'. While this creates methodological problems, especially in connection with his method of intervention, the focus on phenomena transcending the level of organized groups does at least offer an unusual opportunity for the widest possible understanding of collective change in sentiment, values and action. In this respect, Touraine's approach appears to be appropriate for the study of religion above the level of organized groups. This approach could be a valuable complement to the tendency of most sociologists of religion to limit their research either to specific, fully formed organizations or to the attitudes and opinions of individuals. In particular, it would encourage study of the processes whereby general movements in religion, such as evangelicalism or social justice, emerge or fail to emerge fully from lengthy and often confused interaction among participant groups.

The 'old' social movements of industrial society, according to Touraine, were concerned with legal and political problems of production and distribution and were constrained by the thought that there must be an overriding principle of social order such as divine rule, natural law, or the survival of the fittest. But in post-industrial society 'what is crucial now is no longer the struggle between capital and labour in the factory' (Touraine, 1981, p. 6). Instead, the key issue is control over 'the great management and data-processing apparatus' which is allegedly in control of both demand and supply. This apparatus can therefore shape social and cultural behaviour as follows:

Our society invents technologies to produce symbolic goods, languages, information . . . It is already able to transform our body, our sexuality, our mental life. The result is that the field of social movements extends itself to all aspects of social and cultural life. The conclusion is the opposite of the structural Marxist idea according to which social life is controlled by a central agency. The public space, strictly limited in a bourgeois society, was extended to labor problems in an industrial society and now spreads over all fields of experience: private life becomes public, and social scientists who announced some years ago that after a long period of public life, we were withdrawing into private life, did not see that the main political problems today deal directly with private life – fecundation and birth, reproduction and sexuality, illness and death, and, in a different way, with home-consumed mass media.

(Touraine, 1985b, pp. 778–9)

The 'new' social movement is therefore likened to 'class struggle without classes' and, according to Touraine, this could not have occurred in any earlier form of society because it can only develop in post-industrial societies which 'see themselves as the products of their own actions, rather than as part of a process of historical evolution' (Touraine, 1985a, p. 84).

If domination cannot be challenged by appeals to external principles of order, the argument continues, 'only a direct call to personal and collective freedom and responsibility can foster protest movements' (Touraine, 1985b, p. 779). Creativity is the new ideal; utilitarianism is the main obstacle. This is because Touraine defines post-industrial society (or, as he now prefers, the 'programmed' society) not in terms of increased productivity, control and leisure but in terms of 'the technological production of symbolic goods which shape or transform our representations of human nature and of the external world' (Touraine, 1985b, p. 781). The four key components of this model of the programmed society are therefore research and development, information processing, biomedical science and the mass media. This means that, 'society is a system capable of producing, of generating its own normative guidelines instead of having them passed down via an order or a movement that transcends society – no matter whether one call it God, Spirit or History' (Touraine, 1981, p. 14). The fact that the key components are still developing rapidly makes NSMs all the more necessary in Touraine's opinion if these developments are to be shaped and oriented according to values. This is quite reminiscent of the emphasis given by Gramsci to the role of consciousness and political 'will' in combating oppressive social structures.

The fact that Touraine tries to dissociate the kind of normative guidelines that are directly produced by society from 'God, Spirit or History' should not be allowed to conceal the close similarity between his project for *the* social movement and the general objectives of many *religious* movements. In fact, some broad religious movements exhibit precisely the kind of traits which, for Touraine, constitute *the* social movement: a strong sense of distinctive identity for participants, a clear idea of their opponents and a sharp awareness of what is at stake in the movement's struggle against its opponents. Some religious movements could virtually qualify as exemplars of Touraine's notion of social movement in view of their all-encompassing diagnoses of problems and prescriptions for remedies. This is particularly true of so-called norm- and value-oriented religious movements. Indeed, it seems almost perverse and arbitrary for Touraine to deny that such movements as Christian evangelicalism, liberation theology, or Islamic fundamentalism could qualify as social movements. But his reasoning would presumably be that these movements are not self-directing; they follow fixed principles of truth revealed by external sources. Even if they intend to create a new form of society, it would not amount to a truly autonomous creation in Touraine's opinion.

But it is questionable whether *any* social movement could ever fulfil Touraine's conditions. Instead of getting bogged down in definitional disputes, then, it seems preferable to regard Touraine's concept of 'the social movement' as an ideal-type to which actual movements may only approximate in varying degree. This strategy would at least make it possible to conceptualize movements in religion from Touraine's broad perspective and, in this way, to ask questions about their potential contribution to societal development as well as more conventional questions about their social composition or organizational structure. This would be especially valuable in the case of religious movements which adopt an oppositional stance towards the state without transforming themselves into closed, would-be-perfect communities or 'sects', in Touraine's vocabulary. His approach has the merit of making these movements appear less like marginal disputes between different constituencies and more like central struggles for control of the very direction in which post-industrial societies could develop. A further advantage of Touraine's approach is that it discourages exclusive study of concrete movement organizations. Instead, it encourages us to see social movements as emergent and fragmented phenomena which are always in process of looking for their own identity and meaning above and beyond the programme of particular groups or the unfolding of specific conflicts.

DISCUSSION

There are some sharp, if not irreconcilable, differences between the principal theories of NSMs. The movements' historical specificity, relationship to social classes, guiding principles, stance towards the state and potential for progressive change are all contentious issues. This makes it hazardous to offer any substantive generalizations based on the theories. But the theories raise, sometimes by omission, important questions about the changing character of modernity and the equally fluid meaning of religion. They also indicate several points at which attempts to make sociological sense of late capitalism imply that religion and spirituality can be neither dismissed as an irrelevance nor explained in terms of a simplistic theoretical formula.

Habermas, Offe and Touraine all make a point of distinguishing between movements which turn members in on themselves in a search for some revealed or inherited ideal and movements which open members' eyes to the need to take collective responsibility for the direction of social change. They categorize religion as one of the traditional, communitarian and regressive forces. Certainly, most theorists of NSMs reject notions of transcendence and other-worldliness as sources of motivation, solidarity and integration in late-capitalist society. But does this mean that studies of NSMs can have no bearing on religion?

The strongest case for the view that there is, in fact, a religious quality in some NSMs has been made by Melucci (1985, pp. 811–12):

> Contemporary societies have eliminated from the field of human experience what was not measurable and controllable, what in the traditional world belonged to the dimension of the sacred. The final meaning of existence, questions on what escapes individual experience, feed a new 'religious' research or simply a need for

connecting the external change to an interior growth . . .
Movements announce to society that something 'else' is
possible.

Habermas also recognizes that some religious movements may
have a potential for defending the integrity of the life-world in
so far as they 'seek to stem or block' the structures of domination in late-capitalist society. Although religious movements do
not 'seek to conquer new territory', they can nevertheless be
regarded as symptoms of the painful experience of a 'culturally
impoverished and multilaterally rationalized' (Habermas, 1987,
p. 395) life. To repeat a point made earlier, Habermas believes
that 'the establishment and delimitation of communities, the
creation of sub-culturally protected communications groups
which further the search for personal and collective identity'
(Habermas, 1981, p. 36) serve only defensive purposes. They
do not mount an offensive attack on the differentiated social
system. Habermas may, therefore, accept the argument that
religious rituals are among the few occasions on which truly
'serious' things can still be said in secular society (Fenn, 1981)
but he would undoubtedly question whether religious groups
could seriously attack the roots of modern social pathology.
Moreover, although Habermas's theory of late capitalism
draws heavily on social psychological insights into identity,
autonomy and the self, his conclusions are not generally
supportive of movements which merely affirm that 'men
have the right to demand assurance of a sense of personal
worth from society' (Turner, 1969, p. 404). Habermas's more
radical position is that the emancipatory potential of NSMs
lies in their capacity to dictate the future shape of society
on the basis of free and rational discussion among all participants: not simply to demand a larger stake in the present
system.

It seems to me that the kind of communicative action that
underpins Habermas's project for a rational society is indeed
to be found in certain religious movements and in certain
reformist currents within religious organizations. What is
more, many activists in socio-ethical campaigns for human
rights, safeguards for the physical environment and an end

to warfare, for example, have used religious symbolism to good effect. Habermas (1987) has, himself, acknowledged the crucial role of 'sacred' collective representations in everyday social interaction. My conclusion is therefore that his theory of late capitalism and of the strategies which might preserve the benefits of modernity without succumbing to the stultifying effects of a rationalized social system unwittingly provides a justification for taking the changing perceptions of the sacred very seriously. In particular, discourse in various social institutions (law, politics, education, medicine) is centred on issues which raise questions about the definition of what should be regarded as irreducibly 'human' and therefore categorically separate from considerations of material or political advantage. The concept of communicative action, for example, is critical for Habermas's notion of humanity and for the latter's status as sacred in the sense of being categorically beyond question.

With the exception of Melucci, the quasi-Marxist theorists of NSMs seem generally unwilling or unable to conceptualize religion in forms other than that of ecclesiastical or sectarian organizations. In this respect they have largely failed to capitalize fully on the advances that Gramsci made in the understanding of consciousness, ideology and will-formation. This is especially puzzling in view of their professed concern with the centrality of theoretical knowledge, information and cultural values to the late-capitalist mode of production. These theorists also appear to be unaware of the findings of sociological research into, for example, privatized, common, popular and fragmented religion. Even more surprising is their apparent ignorance of Marxist-inspired currents of liberation theology, black theology and feminist theology. It is as if the quasi-Marxist understanding of religion were still rooted in the outmoded concepts of church and sect. As a result, there is an inability to re-frame religion in terms which might show that some of it actually runs in channels which feed into many of the NSMs' preoccupations. Nevertheless, the new and quasi-Marxist theories of late capitalism and of the central importance accorded to new social movements represent a challenge to sociologists of religion. The challenge is to discover whether the theories help to make sense of religious change in general and, if so, how to proceed with research which might clarify the significance of particular religious phenomena in late capitalism.

## NOTE

1   But see the invaluable bibliography in *Social Compass*, 1975, vol. 22, nos. 3–4; and McLellan, 1987.

# Conclusions

The major theoretical contributions to the sociology of religion in the twentieth century fall into three distinct categories. Each of them contains assumptions, definitions, assertions and questions about the nature of religion and social reality.

First, on the assumption that religion functions principally to promote social system integration, social solidarity and social integration, the process of *differentiation* is the most important factor in its development. This covers, for example, the decline of communities, the increase of ethnic complexity, the growth of professional specialisms, the problem of anomie, the development of separate rationalities in different social institutions and the difficulty of finding a shared basis for legitimating the social order.

This powerful problematic has shaped the sociology of religion in innumerable ways but is probably best adapted to studies of relatively slow social change in stable societies. It still dominates the work of most social anthropologists who study religion in pre-industrial societies; and it continues to set the agenda for many sociologists who consider the transition from so-called traditional to industrial society as the paradigm case of modernization. But, with its implicit association between meaning, order, continuity, tradition, community and religion, this problematic has a strong tendency to perceive religion primarily as an endangered species. It therefore runs the risk of conflating historical contingency with categorial necessity for arguing that, since religion *used to be* inseparable from social life in stable communities, the decline of community in the modern world *must* entail the eclipse of 'real' religion.

The advent of highly complex, centralized, planned, diverse, conflictual and rapidly changing societies which take their bearings partly from a virtually global world order puts a strain on this problematic's capacity to make sociological sense of religion today. Niklas Luhmann and some neo-functionalists have, nevertheless, tried to overcome these difficulties, but their insights appear to have been gained at the expense of empirical specificity. The kaleidoscopic, partly contradictory and largely unexpected changes that have taken place in modern religion represent a formidable challenge to those sociologists who still see religion mainly in terms of social system integration, social solidarity and social integration.

Secondly, on the assumption that religion is socially interesting primarily for its capacity to supply *ideas of orderliness, normative guidelines for action and the ultimate grounds for meaning*, the most striking aspects of its modern development include the spread of pluralism and relativism, the rationalization of beliefs and organizations, the persistence of cognitive minorities, and occasional eruptions of charismatic authority.

Like the first problematic, this one was also attuned to the circumstances of an emerging industrial order which undermined many communal bases of belonging or knowing and replaced them with partial social structures sustaining diverse but still plausible systems of meaning. Indeed, the focus on small social worlds, language and micro-interactions has produced valuable insights into the social processes whereby human meaning is generated, negotiated and contested. But a price has been paid for these insights. It is the relative neglect of the wider societal context within which individuals and small social groups construct meanings and values. There has been a reluctance to take serious account of the societal forces which shape and constrain the social construction of meaning.

In particular, the advent of massive state apparatuses of control, the spread of ideological effects through the mass media of communication and the progressive impingement of globe-wide economic, political and ideological forces on individual nation-states call in question the explanatory potential of approaches which tend to isolate social interaction from wider societal forces. To use the example of charisma, it is doubtful whether the phenomenon can be understood nowadays simply in terms of the interactions between a leader and his or her followers. The interactions take place against a background of extensive public relations strategies, commercialism, image management and mass-media hype. In short, no single case of charismatic authority and obedience can nowadays be isolated from these societal conditions.

Finally, on the assumption that the sociological significance of religion lies primarily in its *ideological effects*, i.e. its abillity to disguise the material interests of social classes and class fractions which benefit most from the implantation of religious beliefs, sentiments, values and identities in the minds of exploited classes, the most pressing problems concern the identification of exploiting groups, the understanding of alienation and social conflict, the explanation of religiously based rebellions and the discussion of religion's emancipatory potential.

This particular problematic is most closely tied to ways of theorizing about non-religious topics and, as I argued in Chapter 6, it offers at least the possibility of situating studies of religious or spiritual phenomena firmly in the context of ideas about the class-divided character of industrial, capitalist and post-industrial society. Ironically, however, the tendency has been to focus this problematic on examples from either historical or non-capitalist societies. The persisting liveliness and controversiality of religion in modern and modernizing societies alike therefore represent a major challenge to this largely Marxist problematic. For it is especially well adapted to the task of explaining the place of religion in struggles for power and in social conflicts, but the results have so far been mixed.

Each of these three sets of theoretical problems is rooted in ideas about the transition from pre-industrial to industrial society. These ideas have certainly raised many pertinent questions about the fate of religion in this process, but they now need to be updated or replaced. Although there are significantly different reasons for advocating the use of such terms as 'advanced industrial', 'post-industrial' and 'late capitalist' to describe the key characteristics of societies at the close of the twentieth century, the differences are less important for my purposes than is the deceptively simple fact that we no longer live in industrial societies of the kind depicted by the founding generation of Western sociologists.

The significant changes that have occurred in many aspects of social life since the heyday of industrial society in the West are many and diverse. But no list of them would be complete if it did not contain the following: the growing awareness of the possibility of nuclear annihilation; the emergence of virtually globe-wide norms and points of reference for economic, political and legal/moral practice; the intensification, within the global world order, of massive civil and military conflicts; the aggravation of moral dilemmas arising from the accelerating pace of scientific and technical changes in the extent of control over the human and physical environments; the increasing integration of economic actors in different countries into the same markets and regulatory institutions; the relative decline of manufacturing activity and the growth of service industries; the worsening plight of Third World countries plagued by debts, economic dependency, corruption and militarism; the entry of large numbers of women into the labour force; the deskilling of many workers; the extensive migration from rural to urban areas in developing countries; the increasing frequency of divorce, single parenthood and remarriage; the extension of education to more people; the drop in the average size of households; the spread of rights-based notions of legal process; the growth of single-issue politics; the intensification of gender- and sexual-preference-based advocacy; the concentration of mass-media ownership in fewer corporate hands; rising levels of crime and a decline in the modal age of convicted criminals; the growth of state and international bureaucracies; and the escalating power of leading professions.

At the same time, there are also many continuities between industrial and advanced industrial forms of society. Massive inequalities in power, wealth and well-being are still perpetuated along the lines of social class, gender, ethnicity, race and nationhood; the nation-state remains the most powerful unit of social organization for most purposes; wage labour persists as the most common way of making a living; and representative democracy, in many different guises, has become the most common form of polity.

In the first major reassessments of the sociological meaning of religion in the period after the Second World War when the transition from industrial to advanced industrial began to take place, the dominant themes were that religion would continue to be a force in social life as: the source of values shaping economic and political development; the indispensable medium of socialization; and the inspiration for participation in intermediary associations in the political structures. But many sociologists, by contrast, consigned religion to the margins of the modern world in the form of charismatic cults, social club churches, or communities of ethnic memory.

It is only in the very recent past that a willingness to break away from the limiting problematics of industrial society has led to fresh insights into the new sociological significance of religion. In particular, it is becoming clear that religion can still convey symbols of newly perceived social realities. It can serve as a language for representing powerful inspirations, perceptions, sufferings and aspirations even though the users of this language may not necessarily associate with any religious organization. In some cases, religion conveys conservative ideas of national, tribal, or cultural integrity. In other cases, it conveys new and challenging ideas of personhood, wholeness, peace and justice. In all cases, however, it is apparent that the *use* of religious symbols is likely to be controversial and contested because they are no longer necessarily tied to age-old communities or other so-called natural groupings. It can no longer be taken for granted that most uses of religion will, by definition, be for the straightforward benefit of the whole community. Religion has come adrift from its former points of anchorage but is no less potentially powerful as a result. It remains a potent cultural resource or form which may act as the vehicle of change, challenge, or conservation. Consequently, religion has become less predictable. The capacity to mobilize people and material resources remains strong, but it is likely to be mobilized in unexpected places and in ways which may be in tension with 'establishment' practices and public policy.

This argument about what Simmel might have called the 'autonomization' of religion amounts to much more than the claim that religion can nowadays be marketed in a quasi-commercial fashion. This is only part of the picture. The partial freeing of religion from its points of anchorage in communities and natural social groupings has also turned it into a resource which may be invested with highly diverse meanings and used for a wide variety of purposes. Religion can now be put to varied uses both within and outside the framework of religious organizations and, where they exist, state religions. Civil religions, for example, are best thought of as symbolic resources employed by politicians independently of religious organizations. Religious symbols frequently serve the interests of revolutionaries and political radicals as well. Health care, movements for the protection of the environment or the promotion of peace, and the institutions of human rights are other spheres in which religious symbolism is increasingly being appropriated. The post-Second World War transformation of the kinds of industrial society envisaged by sociologists in the early twentieth century has tended to undermine the communal, familial and organizational bases of religion. But religious forms of sentiment, belief and action have survived as relatively autonomous resources. They retain the capacity to symbolize, for example, ultimate meaning, infinite power, supreme indignation and sublime compassion. And they can be deployed in the service of virtually any interest group or ideal: not just organizations with specifically religious objectives. This presents obvious advantages in states which offer constitutional protections for religious activity. But it also leads to problems if the 'protected' use of religion falls foul of public opinion or government policy (Beckford, 1985).

This can all be summarized in the statement that, from a sociological point of view, it is nowadays better to conceptualize religion as a cultural resource or form than as a social institution. As such, it is characterized by a greater degree of flexibility and unpredictability. For the decline of the great religious monopolies in the West has been accompanied by the sporadic deployment of religion for a great variety of new purposes. Religion can be combined with virtually any other set of ideas or values. And the chances that religion will be controversial are increased by the fact that it may be used by people having little or no connection with formal religious organizations. The deregulation of religion is one of the hidden ironies of secularization. It helps to make religion sociologically problematic in ways which are virtually inconceivable in the terms of the sociological classics.

# References

Abercrombie, N., Hill, S. and Turner, B. S. (1980), *The Dominant Ideology Thesis* (London: Allen & Unwin).

Abercrombie, N., Hill, S. and Turner, B. S. (1986), *Sovereign Individuals of Capitalism* (London: Allen & Unwin).

Acquaviva, S. (1966), *The Decline of the Sacred in Society* (Oxford: Blackwell).

Adler, M. (1925), *Kant und der Marxismus* (Berlin).

Alexander, J. C. (1987), 'The centrality of the classics', in A. Giddens and J. H. Turner (eds), *Social Theory Today* (Oxford: Polity Press), pp. 11–57.

Althusser, L. (1969), *For Marx* (Harmondsworth: Penguin).

Badham, R. (1984), 'The sociology of industrial and post-industrial society', *Current Sociology*, vol. 32, no. 1, pp. 1–157.

Bauer, O. (1927), *Sozialdemokratie, Religion und Kirche* (Vienna).

Becker, H. S. (1957), 'Current sacred–secular theory and its development', in H. Becker and A. Boskoff (eds), *Modern Sociological Theory in Continuity and Change* (New York: Holt, Rinehart & Winston), pp. 133–85.

Beckford, J. A. (1975), 'Religious organization: a trend report and bibliography', *Current Sociology*, vol. 21, no. 2, pp. 1–170.

Beckford, J. A. (1983), 'The restoration of "power" to the sociology of religion', *Sociological Analysis*, vol. 44, no. 1, pp. 11–31.

Beckford, J. A. (1984), 'Holistic imagery and ethics in new religious and healing movements', *Social Compass*, vol. 31, nos. 2–3, pp. 259–72.

Beckford, J. A. (1985), *Cult Controversies: The Societal Response to New Religious Movements* (London: Tavistock).

Bell, D. (1980) 'The return of the sacred?', in D. Bell, *Sociological Journeys, 1960–1980* (London: Heinemann), pp. 324–54.

Bellah, R. N. (1957), *Tokugawa Religion* (New York: Free Press).

Bellah, R. N. (1964), 'Religious evolution', *American Sociological Review*, vol. 29, June, pp. 358–74.

Bellah, R. N. (1967), 'Civil religion in America', *Daedalus*, vol. 96, no. 1, pp. 1–21.

Bellah, R. N. (1970), *Beyond Belief* (New York: Harper & Row).

Bellah, R. N. (1975), *The Broken Covenant. American Civil Religion in Time of Trial* (New York: Seabury Press).

Bellah, R. N. Madsen, R., Sullivan, W. M., Swidler, A. and Tipton, S. M. (1985), *Habits of the Heart. Individualism and Commitment in American Life* (Berkeley, Calif.: University of California Press).

Berger, P. L. (1961a), *The Noise of Solemn Assemblies* (Garden City, NY: Doubleday).

Berger, P. L. (1961b), *The Precarious Vision* (Garden City, NY: Doubleday).

Berger, P. L. (1967), *The Sacred Canopy: Elements of a Sociological Theory of Religion* (Garden City, NY: Doubleday).

Berger, P. L. (1974a), 'Some second thoughts on substantive versus functional definitions of religion', *Journal for the Scientific Study of Religion*, vol. 13, no. 2, pp. 125–33.

Berger, P. L. (1974b), *Pyramids of Sacrifice* (Harmondsworth: Penguin).

Berger, P. L. (1977), *Facing Up to Modernity* (New York: Basic Books).

Berger, P. L. (1983), 'The Third World as a religious idea', *Partisan Review*, vol. 50, no. 2, pp. 183–96.

Berger, P. L. (1986), *The Capitalist Revolution* (New York: Basic Books).

Berger, P. L., Berger, B., and Kellner, H. (1973), *The Homeless Mind* (New York: Random House).

Berger, P. L., and Luckmann, T. (1963) 'Sociology of religion and sociology of knowledge', *Sociology and Social Research*, vol. 47, no. 1, pp. 417–27.

Berger, P. L., and Luckmann, T. (1966a), *The Social Construction of Reality* (Garden City, NY: Doubleday).

Berger, P. L., and Luckmann, T. (1966b), 'Secularization and pluralism', *Internazionales Jahrbuch für Religionssoziologie*, vol. 2, pp. 73–86.

Birnbaum, N. (1955), 'Monarchs and sociologists: a reply to Professor Shils and Mr. Young', *The Sociological Review*, vol. 3, no. 1, pp. 5–23.

Birnbaum, N. (1956), 'La sociologie de la religion en Grande Bretagne', *Archives de Sociologie des Religions*, vol. 2, pp. 3–16.

Boulard, F. and Rémy, J. (1968), *Pratique religieuse urbaine et régions culturelles* (Paris: Editions Ouvrières).

Bourdieu, R. (1971), 'Genèse et structure du champ religieux', *Revue française de Sociologie*, vol. 12, pp. 295–334.

Chidester, D. (1986), 'Michel Foucault and the study of religion', *Religious Studies Review*, vol. 12, no. 1, pp. 1–9.

Comstock, R. (1976), 'The Marxist critique of religion: a persisting ambiguity', *Journal of the American Academy of Religion*, vol. 44, no. 2, pp. 327–42.

Davis, K. (1949), *Human Society* (New York: Macmillan).

Durkheim, E. (1964), *The Division of Labour in Society* (New York: Free Press).

Eisenstadt, S. N. (ed.) (1968), *The Protestant Ethic and Modernization: A Comparative View* (New York: Basic Books).

Eister, A. W. (1957), 'Religious institutions in complex societies: difficulties in the theoretic specification of functions', *American Sociological Review*, vol. 22, no. 4, pp. 387–91.

Eister, A. W. (1973), 'Richard Niebuhr and the paradox of religious organization: a radical critique', in C. Y. Glock and P. E. Hammond (eds), *Beyond the Classics?* (San Francisco: Harper & Row), pp. 476–545.

Faunce, W. A. (1968), *Problems of an Industrial Society* (New York: McGraw-Hill).

Faunce, W. A. and Form, W. H. (1969), *Comparative Perspectives on Industrial Society* (Boston, Mass.: Little, Brown).

Fenn, R. K. (1970), 'The process of secularization: a post-Parsonian view', *Journal for the Scientific Study of Religion*, vol. 9, no. 2, pp. 117–36.

Fenn, R. K. (1972), 'Toward a new sociology of religion', *Journal for the Scientific Study of Religion*, vol. 11, no. 1, pp. 16–32.

Fenn, R. K. (1978), *Toward a Theory of Secularization* (Storrs, Conn.: Society for the Scientific Study of Religion).

Fenn, R. K. (1981), *Liturgies and Trials* (Oxford: Blackwell).

Fenn, R. K. (1982), 'The sociology of religion: a critical survey', in T. Bottomore, S. Nowak and M. Sokolowska (eds), *Sociology: The State of the Art* (London: Sage), pp. 101–27.

Fenn, R. K. (1987), *The Dream of the Perfect Act* (New York: Tavistock).

Foucault, M. (1978), *The History of Sexuality*, Vol. 1, *An Introduction* (New York: Random House).

Foucault, M. (1982), 'The subject and power', in H. L. Dreyfus and P. Rabinow, *Michel Foucault: Beyond Structuralism and Hermeneutics* (Chicago: University of Chicago Press), pp. 208–26.

Gehrig, G. (1981), *American Civil Religion: An Assessment* (Storrs, Conn.: Society for the Scientific Study of Religion).

Godelier, M. (1977), *Perspectives in Marxist Anthropology* (Cambridge: Cambridge University Press).

Goode, W. (1951), *Religion among the Primitives* (Glencoe, Ill.: Free Press).

Gorz, A. (1982), *Farewell to the Working Class* (London: Pluto Press).

Gouldner, A. (1971), *The Coming Crisis of Western Sociology* (London: Heinemann).

Habermas, J. (1981), 'New social movements', *Telos*, vol. 49, Fall, pp. 33–7.

Habermas, J. (1987), *The Theory of Communicative Action*, Vol. 2 (Boston, Mass.: Beacon Press).

Hadden, J. (1987), 'Toward desacralizing secularization theory', *Social Forces*, vol. 65, no. 3, pp. 587–611.

Hammond, P. E. (1980), 'Pluralism and law in the formation of American civil religion', in R. N. Bellah and P. E. Hammond (eds), *Varieties of Civil Religion* (San Francisco: Harper & Row), pp. 138–63.

Harrison, P. M. (1959), *Authority and Power in the Free Church Tradition* (Carbondale, Ill.: Southern Illinois University Press).

Harrison, P. M. (1960), 'Church and laity among Protestants', *Annals of the American Academy of Political and Social Science*, vol. 332, Nov., pp. 37–49.

Herberg, W. (1955), *Protestant-Catholic-Jew* (Garden City, NJ: Doubleday).

Hervieu-Léger, D. (1986), *Vers un nouveau christianisme?* (Paris: Cerf).

Hobhouse, L. T. (1906), *Morals in Evolution* (New York: H. Holt).

Hobhouse, L. T., Wheeler, G. C. and Ginsberg, M. (1915), *The Material Culture and Social Institutions of the Simpler Peoples* (London: Chapman & Hall).

Houtart, F. (1974), *Religion and Ideology in Sri Lanka* (Bangalore: TPI).

Houtart, F., and Lemercinier, G. (1983), 'Conscience religieuse et conscience politique en Amérique Centrale', *Social Compass*, vol. 30, nos. 2–3, pp. 153–74.

Hunter, J. D. (1987), 'Religious elites in advanced industrial society', *Comparative Studies in Society and History*, vol. 29, no. 2, pp. 360–74.

Johnson, B. (1961), 'Do Holiness sects socialize in dominant values?', *Social Forces*, vol. 39, May, pp. 309–16.

Kerr, C., Dunlop, J. T., Harbison, F. H. and Myers, C. A. (1960), *Industrialism and Industrial Man* (Harmondsworth: Penguin).

Lanternari, V. (1963), *The Religions of the Oppressed* (New York: Knopf).

Larrain, J. (1979), *The Concept of Ideology* (London: Hutchinson).

Lenski, G. (1961), *The Religious Factor* (Garden City, NJ: Doubleday).

Leuba, J. H. (1916), *The Belief in God and Immortality* (Boston, Mass.: Sherman, French).

Luckmann, T. (1967), *The Invisible Religion* (New York: Macmillan).

Luhmann, N. (1974), 'Institutionalized religion in the perspective of functional sociology', *Concilium* vol. 1, no. 10, pp. 45–55.

Luhmann, N. (1982), *The Differentiation of Society* (New York: Columbia University Press).

Luhmann, N. (1984), *Religious Dogmatics and the Evolution of Societies* (New York: Edwin Mellen Press).

Luhmann, N. (1987), 'The representation of society within society', *Current Sociology*, vol. 35, no. 2, pp. 101–8.

McLellan, D. (1987), *Marxism and Religion* (London: Macmillan).

Maduro, O. (1977), 'New Marxist approaches to the relative autonomy of religion', *Sociological Analysis*, vol. 38, no. 4, pp. 359–67.

Maduro, O. (1982), *Religion and Social Conflicts* (Maryknoll, NY: Orbis).

Martin, D. A. (1978), *A General Theory of Secularization* (Oxford: Blackwell).

Melucci, A. (1985), 'The symbolic challenge of contemporary movements', *Social Research*, vol. 52, no. 4, pp. 789–816.

Mills, C. Wright (1959), *The Sociological Imagination* (New York: Oxford University Press).

Neal, M.A. (1985), 'Social justice and the sacred', in P. E. Hammond (ed.), *The Sacred in a Secular Age* (Berkeley, Calif.: University of California Press), pp. 333–46.

Niebuhr, H. R. (1929), *The Social Sources of Denominationalism* (New York: Holt, Rinehart & Winston).

Nottingham, E. (1954), *Religion and Society* (Garden City, NJ.: Doubleday).

Nottingham, E. (1971), *Religion: A Sociological View* (New York: Random House).

O'Dea, T. (1963), 'Sociological dilemmas: five paradoxes of institutionalization', in E. Tyriakian (ed.), *Sociological Theory, Values and Sociocultural Change* (London: Free Press), pp. 71–89.

O'Dea, T. (1966), *The Sociology of Religion* (Englewood Cliffs, NJ: Prentice-Hall).

Offe, C. (1984), *Contradictions of the Welfare State* (London: Hutchinson).

Offe, C. (1985), 'New social movements: challenging the boundaries of institutional politics', *Social Research*, vol. 52, no. 4, pp. 817–68.

Opazo Bernales, A. (1983), 'Les conditions sociales du surgissement d'une église populaire', *Social Compass*, vol. 30, nos. 2–3, pp. 175–209.

O'Toole, R. (1984), *Religion: Classic Sociological Approaches* (Toronto: McGraw-Hill, Ryerson).

Parsons, T. (1937), *The Structure of Social Action* (New York: McGraw-Hill).

Parsons, T. (1951), *The Social System* (New York: Free Press).

Parsons, T. (1958), 'Réflexions sur les organizations religieuses aux Etats-Unis', *Archives de Sociologie des Religions*, Jan-June 1958, pp. 21–36; extended and translated as 'The pattern of religious organization in the United States', *Daedalus*, Summer 1968, pp. 65–85.

Parsons, T. (1960a), 'Some principal characteristics of industrial societies', in T. Parsons, *Structure and Process in Modern Society* (New York: Free Press), pp. 132–68.

Parsons, T. (1960b), 'Some comments on the pattern of religious organization in the United States', in T. Parsons *Structure and Process in Modern Society* (New York: Free Press), pp. 295–321.

Parsons, T. (1960c), 'Mental illness and "spiritual malaise": the roles of the psychiatrist and of the minister of religion', in H. Hofmann (ed.), *The Ministry and Mental Health* (New York: Association Press), pp. 23–47.

Parsons, T. (1966), *Societies. Evolutionary and Comparative Perspectives* (Englewood Cliffs, NJ: Prentice-Hall).

Parsons, T. (1968), 'On the concept of value-commitments', *Sociological Inquiry*, vol. 38, no. 2, pp. 135–60.

Parsons, T. (1974), 'Religion in postindustrial America: the problem of secularization', *Social Research*, vol. 41, no. 2, pp. 193–225.

Parsons, T. and Shils E. (eds) (1951), *Toward a General Theory of Action* (Cambridge, Mass.: Harvard University Press).

Pfautz, H. W. (1956), 'Christian Science: a case study of the social psychological aspect of secularization', *Social Forces*, vol. 34, pp. 246–51.

Plath, D. (1966), 'The fate of Utopia: adaptive tactics in four Japanese groups', *American Anthropologist*, vol. 68, no. 2, pp. 1152–62.

Poblete, R. (1960), 'A sociological approach to the sects', *Social Compass*, vol. 1, nos. 5–6, pp. 383–406.

Pope, L. (1942), *Millhands and Preachers* (New Haven, Conn.: Yale University Press).

Prendes, J. C. (1983), 'Revolutionary struggle and church commitment: the case of El Salvador', *Social Compass*, vol. 30, nos. 2–3, pp. 261–98.

Reed, M. (1981), 'An alliance for progress: the early years of the sociology of religion in the United States', *Sociological Analysis*, vol. 42, no. 1, pp. 27–46.

Robbins, T. (1983), 'The beach is washing away: controversial religion and the sociology of religion', *Sociological Analysis*, vol. 44, no. 3, pp. 207–14.

Robbins, T., and Robertson R. (eds.) (1987) *Church–State Relations. Tensions and Transitions* (New Brunswick, NJ: Transaction Books).

Robertson, R. (1985a), 'Beyond the sociology of religion?', *Sociological Analysis*, vol. 46, no. 4, pp. 355–60.

Robertson, R. (1985b) 'The sacred and the world system', in P. E. Hammond (ed), *The Sacred in a Secular Age* (Berkeley, Calif.: University of California Press), pp. 347–58.

Robertson, R. (1987), 'General considerations in the study of contemporary church–state relations', in Robbins and Robertson, op. cit., pp. 5–11.

Robertson, R., and Chirico J. (1985) 'Humanity, globalization and worldwide religious resurgence: a theoretical exploration', *Sociological Analysis*, vol. 46, no. 3, pp. 219–42.

Schöfthaler, T. (1984), 'The social foundations of morality: Durkheimian problems and the vicissitudes of Niklas Luhmann's systems theories of religion, morality and personality', *Social Compass*, vol. 31, nos. 2–3, pp. 185–97.

Séguy, J. (1980), *Christianisme et Société. Introduction à la Sociologie de Ernst Troeltsch* (Paris: Cerf).

Séguy, J. (1985), 'Charisma in the modern world', in *Acts of the 18th International Conference for the Sociology of Religion* (Lausanne: Conférence Internationale de la Sociologie des Religions), pp. 51–65.

Shils, E. (1975), *Center and Periphery* (Chicago: University of Chicago Press).

Steeman, T. (1984), 'Troeltsch and modern American religion', *Archives de Sciences sociales des Religions*, vol. 58, no. 1, pp. 85–116.

Swatos W. (1984), *Faith of the Fathers: Science, Religion, and Reform in the Development of Early American Sociology* (Bristol, Ind.: Windham Hall Press).

Terray, E. (1972), *Marxism and 'Primitive Societies'* (New York: Monthly Review Press); 1st edn, 1969.

Thompson, K. (1986), *Beliefs and Ideology* (Chichester: Ellis Horwood).

Touraine, A. (1981), *The Voice and the Eye* (Cambridge: Cambridge University Press); 1st edn, 1978.

Touraine, A. (1985a), 'Social movements and social change', in O. Fals Borda (ed.), *The Challenge of Social Change* (London: Sage), pp. 77–92.

Touraine, A. (1985b), 'An introduction to the study of social movements', *Social Research*, vol. 52, no. 4, pp. 749–87.

Turner, B. S. (1983), *Religion and Social Theory* (London: Heinemann).

Turner, R. (1969), 'The theme of contemporary social movements', *British Journal of Sociology*, vol. 20, no. 4, pp. 390–405.

Tyriakian, E. (1981), 'Durkheim's "elementary forms" as "revelation"', in B. Rhea (ed.), *The Future of the Sociological Classics* (London: Allen & Unwin), pp. 114–35.

Vidich, A. J. and Lyman S. M. (1985), *American Sociology* (New Haven, Conn.: Yale University Press).

Vrcan, S. (1977), 'Working-class commitment to religion and church in Yugoslavia', in *Acts of the 14th International Conference for the Sociology of Religion* (Lille: Conférence Internationale de la Sociologie des Religions), pp. 327–47.

Westermaarck, E. (1906), *The Origin and Development of Moral Ideas*, 2 vols. (London: Macmillan).

Wilson, B. R. (1975), *The Noble Savages. The Primitive Origins of Charisma and its Contemporary Survival* (Berkeley, Calif.: University of California Press).

Wilson, B. R. (1976), *Contemporary Transformations of Religion* (London: Oxford University Press).

Wilson, B. R. (1979), 'The return of the sacred', *Journal for the Scientific Study of Religion*, vol. 18, no. 3, pp. 268–80.

Wilson, B. R. (1982), *Religion in Sociological Perspective* (Oxford: Oxford University Press).

Wuthnow, R. (1986), 'Religious movements and countermovements in North America', in J. A. Beckford (ed.), *New Religious Movements and Rapid Social Change* (London: Sage), pp. 1–28.

Wuthnow, R. (1988), *The Restructuring of American Religion* (Princeton, NJ: Princeton University Press).

Yinger, J. M. (1946), *Religion in the Struggle for Power* (Durham, NC: Duke University Press).

Zald, M. (1970), *Organizational Change: The Political Economy of the YMCA* (Chicago: University of Chicago Press).

Zijderveld, A. (1970), *The Abstract Society* (Harmondsworth: Penguin).

# Index